THE CHURCH
TOWARDS A COMMON VISION

Faith and Order Paper No. 214

World Council of Churches
Publications

THE CHURCH
Towards a Common Vision
Faith and Order Paper No. 214

WCC Publications is the book publishing programme of the World Council of Churches. Founded in 1948, the WCC promotes Christian unity in faith, witness and service for a just and peaceful world. A global fellowship, the WCC brings together more than 349 Protestant, Orthodox, Anglican and other churches representing more than 560 million Christians in 110 countries and works cooperatively with the Roman Catholic Church.

Scripture quotations are from the New Revised Standard Version Bible, © copyright 1989 by the Division of Christian Education of the National Council of the Churches of Christ in the USA. Used by permission.

Cover design: GPS Publishing
Book design and typesetting: GPS Publishing
ISBN: 978-2-8254-1587-0

World Council of Churches
150 route de Ferney, P.O. Box 2100
1211 Geneva 2, Switzerland
http://publications.oikoumene.org

CONTENTS

Chapter IV - The Church: In and for the World **33**

Conclusion (67-69) 39

Historical Note: The Process Leading to The Church: Towards a Common Vision *41*

Foreword

In my visits to the churches around the world, I am introduced to many challenges to the unity between and within the churches. The many ecumenical dialogues between churches and church families are a reality that contributes also to the multilateral relationships between them. New connections are established thereby. However, there is a certain and reasonable impatience among many to see more movement in the reception of ecumenical dialogues and agreements. Some of the churches and families of churches find that there are also new questions that are potentially dividing. The ecumenical movement seems also in some churches to have less power and fewer committed spokespersons than in earlier periods. There are tendencies toward fragmentation and more attention to what is uniting the few rather than the many. Of course, the call to unity is not ended by new challenges, rather the contrary. Yet we also need to see more dimensions of the call to unity and remind ourselves that we are always embraced by and called to love (1 Cor. 13).

Into this context the WCC's Commission on Faith and Order presents to us a gift, a statement about the

Church: it is a fruit of their many years of work on ecclesiology. Stemming from *Baptism, Eucharist and Ministry* (1982) and the churches' responses to it, *The Church: Towards a Common Vision* was received by the central committee in 2012 and sent to the churches to encourage further reflection on the Church and to seek their formal responses to the text. This study and its response process will have an important role in the coming years for discerning the next steps toward visible unity. Work on ecclesiology relates to everything the Church is and what its mission implies in and for the world. Thus, *The Church* is rooted in the nature and mission of the Church. It reflects the constitutional aims and self-identity of the WCC as a fellowship of churches who call each other to the goal of visible unity.

Unity is a gift of life and a gift of love, not a principle of unanimity or unilateralism. We have a calling as a fellowship of churches to express the unity of life that is given to us in Jesus Christ, through his life, cross and resurrection so that brokenness, sin, and evil can be overcome. For as *The Church* proclaims: "The kingdom of God, which Jesus preached by revealing the Word of God in parables and inaugurated by his mighty deeds, especially by the paschal mystery of his death and resurrection, is the final destiny of the whole universe. The Church was intended by God, not for its own sake, but to serve the divine plan for the transformation of the world" (§ 58).

Olav Fykse Tveit
General Secretary
World Council of Churches

Preface

The convergence text *The Church: Towards a Common Vision* belongs to the biblical vision of Christian unity: "For just as the body is one and has many members, and all the members of the body, though many, are one body, so it is with Christ. For in the one Spirit we were all baptized into one body—Jews or Greeks, slaves or free—and we were all made to drink of one Spirit" (1 Cor. 12:12-13).

The primary purpose of the Commission on Faith and Order is "to serve the churches as they call one another to visible unity in one faith and in one Eucharistic fellowship, expressed in worship and common life in Christ, through witness and service to the world, and advance towards that unity in order that the world may believe" (2012 bylaws).

The goal of this mutual calling to visible unity necessarily entails a mutual recognition of each other as churches, as true expressions of what the Creed calls the "one, holy, catholic and apostolic Church." Yet in the abnormal situation of ecclesial division, the churches' reflection on the nature and mission of the Church has given rise to the suspicion that the various confessional ecclesiologies are not only divergent from one another but also irreconcilable. Hence agreement on ecclesiology has long been identified as the most elemental theological objective in the quest for Christian unity. This second convergence text of Faith and Order follows from the first, *Baptism, Eucharist and Ministry* (1982), and the official responses to it, which identified key areas in ecclesiology for further study;[1] it follows as well from the ecclesiological questions raised in the study text *One Baptism: Towards Mutual Recognition* (2011).

For twenty years, the delegated representatives of the Orthodox, Protestant, Anglican, Evangelical, Pentecostal and Roman Catholic churches in a World Conference on Faith and Order (1993), three Plenary Commissions on Faith and Order (1996, 2004, 2009), eighteen meetings of the Standing Commission, and countless drafting meetings have sought to uncover a global, multilateral and ecumenical vision of the nature, purpose, and mission of the Church. The churches have responded critically and constructively to two earlier stages on the way to a common statement. The Commission on Faith and Order responds to the churches with *The Church: Towards a Common Vision*, its common – or convergence – statement on ecclesiology. The convergence reached in *The Church* represents an extraordinary ecumenical achievement.

There are at least two distinct, but deeply interrelated, objectives in sending *The Church* to the churches for study and official response. The first is renewal. As a multilateral ecumenical text, *The Church* cannot be identified exclusively with any one ecclesiological tradition. In the long process from 1993-2012, the theological expressions and ecclesial experiences of many churches have been brought together in such a way that the churches reading this text may find themselves challenged to live more fully the ecclesial life; others may find in it aspects of ecclesial life and understanding which have been neglected or forgotten; others may find themselves strengthened and affirmed. As Christians experience life-long growth into Christ, they will find themselves drawing closer to one another, and living into the biblical image of the one body: "For in the one Spirit we were all baptized into one body – Jews or Greeks, slaves or free – and we were all made to drink of one Spirit."

The second objective is theological agreement on the Church. As important as the convergence achieved by Faith and Order in *Baptism, Eucharist and Ministry* was the official response process that followed. The six published volumes of responses manifested the varying levels of documented convergences among the churches themselves on the key questions around baptism, eucharist and ministry. The effects of the ecclesial convergence surfaced by *Baptism, Eucharist and Ministry* toward Christian unity are well-documented and ongoing. The responses to *The Church: Towards a Common Vision* will not only evaluate the convergence reached by Faith and Order but also reflect the level of convergence on ecclesiology among the churches. Just as the convergence on baptism in the responses to *Baptism, Eucharist and Ministry* gave rise to a fresh impetus toward mutual recognition of baptism, similar ecclesial convergence on ecclesiology will play a vital role in the mutual recognition between the churches as they call one another to visible unity in one faith and in one eucharistic fellowship.

"Ecclesial responses" for the Commission on Faith and Order includes the churches that are members of the Commission and the fellowship of churches in the

---

[1] Cf. *Baptism, Eucharist & Ministry, 1982-1990: Report on the Process and Responses.* Faith and Order Paper No. 149. WCC: Geneva, 1990, 147-151.

World Council of Churches. It is also hoped that those churches that are new to the ecumenical movement will accept the invitation to study and comment on the text. The Commission also welcomes responses from ecclesial bodies, such as national and regional councils of churches and the Christian World Communions, whose official dialogues among themselves have contributed so much to the convergence reflected in *The Church*. The specific questions posed by Faith and Order to the churches to guide their response process are found at the end of the Introduction to *The Church*. The questions for study and response are theological, practical, and pastoral. The Commission requests that official responses be sent to the Faith and Order secretariat at the World Council of Churches no later than 31 December 2015.

As this text was two decades in the making, we express our thanks to those on whose shoulders, prayers and theological gifts this text stands: the Faith and Order commissioners, the churches and theologians who responded to *The Nature and Purpose of the Church* (1998) and *The Nature and Mission of the Church* (2005), members of the Faith and Order secretariat, and our own predecessors as moderators and directors of the Commission on Faith and Order.

Canon John Gibaut
Director
Commission on
Faith and Order

Metropolitan Dr Vasilios
of Constantia-Ammochostos
Moderator
Commission on
Faith and Order

INTRODUCTION

"Thy will be done" are words that countless believers from all Christian churches pray every day. Jesus himself prayed similar words in the garden of Gethsemane shortly before his arrest (cf. Matt. 26:39-42; Mark 14:36; Luke 22:42). In John's gospel, moreover, he revealed his will for the Church when he prayed to the Father that all of his disciples be one, so that the world may believe (cf. John 17:21). To pray that the Lord's will be done thus necessarily requires a wholehearted endeavour to embrace his will for and gift of unity. The present text – *The Church: Towards a Common Vision* – addresses what many consider to be the most difficult issues facing the churches in overcoming any remaining obstacles to their living out the Lord's gift of communion: our understanding of the nature of the Church itself. The great importance of that gift and goal highlights the significance of the issues to be treated in the pages that follow.

Our aim is to offer a convergence text, that is, a text which, while not expressing full consensus on all the issues considered, is much more than simply an instrument to stimulate further study. Rather, the following pages express how far Christian communities have come in their common understanding of the Church, showing the progress that has been made and indicating work that still needs to be done. The present text has been elaborated by the Faith and Order Commission, whose aim, like that of the World Council of Churches as a whole, is to serve the churches as they "call one another to visible unity in one faith and one eucharistic fellowship, expressed in worship and common life in Christ, through witness and service to the world, and to advance towards that unity in order that the world may believe."[1] Such visible unity finds a most eloquent expression in the celebration of the eucharist, which glorifies the Triune God and enables the Church to participate in the mission of God for the transformation and salvation of the world. The present statement makes use of the responses of the churches to Faith and Order's work on ecclesiology in recent years as well as earlier ecumenical documents which have sought convergence through common reflection upon God's Word, in the hope that, under the guidance of the Holy Spirit, the Lord's gift of unity can be fully realized. Thus it is the result of dialogue at the multilateral level, especially the responses of the churches to *The Nature and Mission of the Church*, of the suggestions offered by the meeting of the Faith and Order plenary commission held in Crete in 2009 and of the contributions of the Orthodox consultation held in Cyprus in 2011. In addition, the text draws upon the progress registered in many bilateral dialogues that have taken up the theme of "Church" in recent decades.[2]

We hope that *The Church: Towards a Common Vision* will serve the churches in three ways: (1) by providing a synthesis of the results of ecumenical dialogue about important ecclesiological themes in recent decades; (2) by inviting them to appraise the results of this dialogue – confirming positive achievements, pointing out deficiencies and/or indicating areas that have not received sufficient attention; and (3) by providing an occasion for the churches to reflect upon their own understanding of the Lord's will so as to grow towards greater unity (cf. Eph. 4:12-16). Hopefully, such a process of information, reaction and growth, by confirming, enriching and challenging all of the churches, will make a substantial contribution and even enable some decisive steps towards the full realization of unity.

There is a structure to this text, based on the ecclesiological issues that we are addressing. *The Church: Towards a Common Vision* opens with a chapter exploring how the Christian community finds its origin in the mission of God for the saving transformation of the world. The Church is essentially missionary, and unity is essentially related to this mission. The second chapter sets out the salient features of an understanding of the Church as Communion, gathering the results of much common reflection both about how Scripture and subsequent tradition relate the Church to God and some of the consequences of this relation for the life and structure of the Church. The third chapter focuses upon the growth of the Church as the pilgrim people moving towards the kingdom of God, especially upon several difficult ecclesiological questions that have divided the churches in the past. It registers the progress towards greater convergence about some of these issues and clarifies points about which churches may need to seek further convergence. The fourth chapter develops several significant ways in which the Church relates to the world as a sign and agent of God's love, such as proclaiming Christ within an interreligious context, witnessing to the moral values of the Gospel and responding to human suffering and need.

The many official responses to Faith and Order's *Baptism, Eucharist and Ministry*, of 1982, showed that the process of reception that follows the publication of a convergence text can prove to be just as important as that

---

[1] L. N. Rivera-Pagán (ed.), *God in Your Grace: Official Report of the Ninth Assembly of the World Council of Churches*, Geneva, WCC, 2007, 448.
[2] For more details about this process, see the historical note which appears at the end of the text.

which led to its production.[3] So as to serve as an instrument for genuine dialogue about ecclesiology to which all may make a significant contribution, the churches are urgently requested not only to give serious consideration to *The Church: Towards a Common Vision* but also to submit an official response to the Faith and Order Commission, in the light of the following questions:

- To what extent does this text reflect the ecclesiological understanding of your church?

- To what extent does this text offer a basis for growth in unity among the churches?

- What adaptations or renewal in the life of your church does this statement challenge your church to work for?

- How far is your church able to form closer relationships in life and mission with those churches which can acknowledge in a positive way the account of the Church described in this statement?

- What aspects of the life of the Church could call for further discussion and what advice could your church offer for the ongoing work by Faith and Order in the area of ecclesiology?

In addition to these general questions, readers will find, printed in italics and interspersed throughout the text, paragraphs about specific issues where divisions remain. These questions are intended to stimulate reflection and encourage further agreement among the churches on the path to unity.

---

[3] M. Thurian (ed.), *Churches Respond to BEM: Official Responses to the "Baptism, Eucharist and Ministry" Text*, Geneva, World Council of Churches, vols. I-VI, 1986-1988; *Baptism, Eucharist & Ministry 1982-1990: Report on the Process and Responses*, Geneva, WCC, 1990.

CHAPTER I

God's Mission and the Unity of the Church

A. The Church in the Design of God

1. The Christian understanding of the Church and its mission is rooted in the vision of God's great design (or "economy") for all creation: the "kingdom" which was both promised by and manifested in Jesus Christ. According to the Bible, man and woman were created in God's image (cf. Gen. 1:26-27), so bearing an inherent capacity for communion (in Greek *koinonia*) with God and with one another. God's purpose in creation was thwarted by human sin and disobedience (cf. Gen. 3-4; Rom. 1:18-3:20), which damaged the relationship between God, human beings and the created order. But God persisted in faithfulness despite human sin and error. The dynamic history of God's restoration of *koinonia* found its irreversible achievement in the incarnation and paschal mystery of Jesus Christ. The Church, as the body of Christ, acts by the power of the Holy Spirit to continue his life-giving mission in prophetic and compassionate ministry and so participates in God's work of healing a broken world. Communion, whose source is the very life of the Holy Trinity, is both the gift by which the Church lives and, at the same time, the gift that God calls the Church to offer to a wounded and divided humanity in hope of reconciliation and healing.

2. During his earthly ministry, "Jesus went throughout all the cities and villages, teaching in their synagogues and proclaiming the gospel of the kingdom

and healing every disease and every sickness. When he saw the crowds he had compassion for them..." (Matt. 9:35-36). The Church takes its mandate from the act and promise of Christ himself, who not only proclaimed the kingdom of God in word and deed but also called men and women and sent them out, empowered by the Holy Spirit (John 20:19-23). The Acts of the Apostles tell us that the last words Jesus addressed to the apostles before his ascension into heaven were: "You will receive power when the Holy Spirit has come upon you; and you will be my witnesses in Jerusalem, in all Judea and Samaria, and to the end of the earth" (Acts 1:8). Each of the four gospels closes with a missionary mandate; Matthew recounts: "And Jesus came and said to them, 'All authority in heaven and on earth has been given to me. Go therefore and make disciples of all nations, baptizing them in the name of the Father and of the Son and of the Holy Spirit, teaching them to observe all that I have commanded you; and lo, I am with you always, to the close of the age'" (Matt. 28:18-20; see also Mark 16:15; Luke 24:45-49; John 20:19-21). This command by Jesus already hints at what he wanted his Church to be in order to carry out this mission. It was to be a community of witness, proclaiming the kingdom which Jesus had first proclaimed, inviting human beings from all nations to saving faith. It was to be a community of worship, initiating new members by baptism in the name of the Holy Trinity. It was to be a community of discipleship, in which the apostles, by proclaiming the Word, baptizing and celebrating the Lord's Supper, were to guide new believers to observe all that Jesus himself had commanded.

3. The Holy Spirit came upon the disciples on the morning of Pentecost for the purpose of equipping them to begin the mission entrusted to them (cf. Acts 2:1-41). God's plan to save the world (sometimes referred to with the Latin expression *missio Dei* or "the mission of God"), is carried out through the sending of the Son and the Holy Spirit. This saving activity of the Holy Trinity is essential to an adequate understanding of the Church. As the Faith and Order study document *Confessing the One Faith* pointed out: "Christians believe and confess with the Creed that there is an indissoluble link between the work of God in Jesus Christ through the Holy Spirit and the *reality* of the Church. This is the testimony of the Scriptures. The origin of the Church is rooted in the plan of the Triune God for humankind's salvation."[1]

4. Jesus described his ministry as preaching the good news to the poor, releasing the captives, giving sight to the blind, liberating the oppressed and proclaiming the acceptable year of the Lord (cf. Luke 4:18-19, quoting Is. 61:1-2). "The mission of the Church ensues from the nature of the Church as the body of Christ, sharing in the ministry of Christ as Mediator between God and his creation. At the heart of the Church's vocation in the world is the proclamation of the kingdom of God inaugurated in Jesus the Lord, crucified and risen. Through its internal life of eucharistic worship, thanksgiving, intercessory prayer, through planning for mission and evangelism, through a daily life-style of solidarity with the poor, through advocacy even to confrontation with the powers that oppress human beings, the churches are trying to fulfil this evangelistic vocation."[2]

---

[1] *Confessing the One Faith: An Ecumenical Explication of the Apostolic Faith as It Is Confessed in the Nicene-Constantinopolitan Creed (381)*, Geneva-Eugene, WCC-Wipf & Stock, 2010, §216.

[2] "Mission and Evangelism: An Ecumenical Affirmation," §6, in J. Matthey (ed.), *You Are the Light of the World: Statements on Mission by the World Council of Churches*, Geneva, WCC, 2005, 8.

B. The Mission of the Church in History

5. Since these origins, the Church has always been dedicated to proclaiming in word and deed the good news of salvation in Christ, celebrating the sacraments, especially the eucharist, and forming Christian communities. This effort has sometimes encountered bitter resistance; it has sometimes been hindered by opponents or even betrayed by the sinfulness of the messengers. In spite of such difficulties, this proclamation has produced great fruit (cf. Mark 4:8, 20, 26-32).

6. One challenge for the Church has been how to proclaim the Gospel of Christ in a way that awakens a response in the different contexts, languages and cultures of the people who hear that proclamation. St Paul's preaching of Christ in the Areopagus at Athens (Acts 17:22-34), making use of local beliefs and literature, illustrates how the very first generation of Christians attempted to share the good news of Jesus' death and resurrection, drawing upon and, when necessary, transforming, under the guidance of the Holy Spirit, the cultural heritage of their listeners and serving as a leaven to foster the well-being of the society in which they lived. Over the centuries, Christians have witnessed to the Gospel within ever increasing horizons, from Jerusalem to the ends of the earth (cf. Acts 1:8). Often their witness to Jesus resulted in martyrdom, but it also led to the spread of the faith and to the establishment of the Church in every corner of the earth. At times, the cultural and religious heritage of those to whom the Gospel was proclaimed was not given the respect it deserved, as when those engaging in evangelization were complicit in imperialistic colonization, which pillaged and even exterminated peoples unable to defend themselves from more powerful invading nations. Notwithstanding such tragic events, God's grace, more powerful than human sinfulness, was able to raise up true disciples and friends of Christ in many lands and establish the Church within the rich variety of many cultures. Such diversity within the unity of the one Christian community was understood by some early writers as an expression of the beauty which Scripture attributes to the bride of Christ (cf. Eph. 5:27 and Rev. 21:2).[3] Today believers from churches which once welcomed foreign missionaries have been able to come to the assistance of churches by whose agency they first heard the Gospel.[4]

7. Today the proclamation of the kingdom of God continues throughout the world within rapidly changing circumstances. Some developments are particularly challenging to the Church's mission and self-understanding. The widely diffused awareness of religious pluralism challenges Christians to deepen their reflection about the relation between the proclamation that Jesus is the one and only Saviour of the world, on the one hand, and the claims of other faiths, on the other. The development of means of communication challenges the churches to seek new ways to proclaim the Gospel and to establish and maintain Christian communities. The "emerging churches," which propose a new way of being the Church, challenge other churches to find ways of responding to today's needs and interests in ways which are faithful to what has been received from the beginning. The advance of a global secular culture challenges the Church with a situation in which many question the very possibility of faith, believing that human life is sufficient unto itself, without any reference to God. In some places, the Church faces

---

[3] See, for example, Augustine, "Ennarrationes in Psalmos," 44, 24-25, in J. P. Migne, *Patrologia Latina* 36, 509-510.
[4] Such solidarity of mutual assistance is to be clearly distinguished from proselytism, which wrongly considers other Christian communities as a legitimate field for conversion.

the challenge of a radical decline in membership and is perceived by many as no longer relevant to their lives, leading those who still believe to speak of the need for a re-evangelization. All churches share the task of evangelization in the face of these challenges and others that may arise within particular contexts.

C. The Importance of Unity

8. The importance of Christian unity to the mission and nature of the Church was already evident in the New Testament. In Acts 15 and Galatians 1-2, it is clear that the mission to the Gentiles gave birth to tensions and threatened to create divisions between Christians. In a way, the contemporary ecumenical movement is reliving the experience of that first council of Jerusalem. The present text is an invitation to the leaders, theologians and faithful of all churches to seek the unity for which Jesus prayed on the eve before he offered his life for the salvation of the world (cf. John 17:21).

9. Visible unity requires that churches be able to recognize in one another the authentic presence of what the Creed of Nicaea-Constantinople (381) calls the "one, holy, catholic, apostolic Church." This recognition, in turn, may in some instances depend upon changes in doctrine, practice and ministry within any given community. This represents a significant challenge for churches in their journey towards unity.

10. Currently, some identify the Church of Christ exclusively with their own community, while others would acknowledge in communities other than their own a real but incomplete presence of the elements which make up the Church. Others have joined into various types of covenant relationships, which sometimes include the sharing of worship.[5] Some believe that the Church of Christ is located in all communities that present a convincing claim to be Christian, while others maintain that Christ's church is invisible and cannot be adequately identified during this earthly pilgrimage.

Fundamental issues on the way to unity

Ever since the Toronto Declaration of 1950, the WCC has challenged the churches to "recognize that the membership of the church of Christ is more inclusive than the membership of their own church body." Moreover, mutual regard between churches and their members has been profoundly encouraged and advanced by ecumenical encounter. Nevertheless, differences on some basic questions remain and need to be faced together: "How can we identify the Church which the creed calls one, holy, catholic and apostolic?" "What is God's will for the unity of this Church?" "What do we need to do to put God's will into practice?" This text has been written in order to assist the churches as they reflect upon such questions, seeking common answers.[6]

---

[5] Cf. the Anglican-Lutheran report "Growth in Communion," in J. Gros, FSC, T.F. Best and L. F. Fuchs, SA (eds.), *Growth in Agreement III: International Dialogue Texts and Agreed Statements,* 1998-2005, Geneva-Grand Rapids, WCC-Eerdmans, 2007, 375-425, which refers to important Anglican-Lutheran regional covenants (Meissen, Reuilly, Waterloo, etc.).

[6] Thus the present text hopes to build upon the unity statement of the Porto Alegre General Assembly of the World Council of Churches entitled "Called to Be One Church," whose subtitle is "An Invitation to the Churches to Renew Their Commitment to the Search for Unity and to Deepen Their Dialogue," in *Growth in Agreement* III, 606-610. See "Final Report of the Special Commission on Orthodox Participation in the WCC," section III, 12-21, in *Ecumenical Review* 55.1, January 2003, 7-8.

CHAPTER II
The Church of the Triune God

A. Discerning God's Will for the Church

11. All Christians share the conviction that Scripture is normative, therefore the biblical witness provides an irreplaceable source for acquiring greater agreement about the Church. Although the New Testament provides no systematic ecclesiology, it does offer accounts of the faith of the early communities, of their worship and practice of discipleship, of various roles of service and leadership, as well as images and metaphors used to express the identity of the Church. Subsequent interpretation within the Church, seeking always to be faithful to biblical teaching, has produced an additional wealth of ecclesiological insights over the course of history. The same Holy Spirit who guided the earliest communities in producing the inspired biblical text continues, from generation to generation, to guide later followers of Jesus as they strive to be faithful to the Gospel. This is what is understood by the "living Tradition" of the Church.[1] The great importance of Tradition has been acknowledged by most communities, but they vary in assessing how its authority relates to that of Scripture.

---

[1] As the fourth World Conference on Faith and Order pointed out in its report "Scripture, Tradition and Traditions," "By *the Tradition* is meant the Gospel itself, transmitted from generation to generation in and by the Church, Christ himself present in the life of the Church. By *tradition* is meant the traditionary process. The term *traditions* is used ... to indicate both the diversity of forms of expression and also what we call confessional traditions...." P. C. Roger and L. Vischer (eds.), *The Fourth World Conference on Faith and Order: Montreal 1963*, London, SCM Press, 1964, 50. See also *A Treasure in Earthen Vessels: An Instrument for an Ecumenical Reflection on Hermeneutics*, Geneva, WCC, 1998, §§14-37, pages 14-26.

12. A wide variety of ecclesiological insights can be found in the various books of the New Testament and in subsequent Tradition. The New Testament canon, by embracing this plurality, testifies to its compatibility with the unity of the Church, though without denying the limits to legitimate diversity.[2] Legitimate diversity is not accidental to the life of the Christian community but is rather an aspect of its catholicity, a quality that reflects the fact that it is part of the Father's design that salvation in Christ be incarnational and thus "take flesh" among the various peoples to whom the Gospel is proclaimed. An adequate approach to the mystery of the Church requires the use and interaction of a wide range of images and insights (people of God, body of Christ, temple of the Holy Spirit, vine, flock, bride, household, soldiers, friends and so forth). The present text seeks to draw upon the richness of the biblical witness, along with insights from the Tradition.

B. The Church of the Triune God as *Koinonia*

The Initiative of God, the Father, the Son and the Holy Spirit

13. The Church is called into being by the God who "so loved the world that he gave his only Son, so that everyone who believes in him may not perish, but may have eternal life" (John 3:16) and who sent the Holy Spirit to lead these believers into all truth, reminding them of all that Jesus taught (cf. John 14:26). In the Church, through the Holy Spirit, believers are united with Jesus Christ and thereby share a living relationship with the Father, who speaks to them and calls forth their trustful response. The biblical notion of *koinonia* has become central in the ecumenical quest for a common understanding of the

life and unity of the Church. This quest presupposes that communion is not simply the union of existing churches in their current form. The noun *koinonia* (communion, participation, fellowship, sharing), which derives from a verb meaning "to have something in common," "to share," "to participate," "to have part in" or "to act together," appears in passages recounting the sharing in the Lord's Supper (cf. 1 Cor. 10:16-17), the reconciliation of Paul with Peter, James and John (cf. Gal. 2:7-10), the collection for the poor (cf. Rom. 15:26; 2 Cor. 8:3-4) and the experience and witness of the Church (cf. Acts 2:42-45). As a divinely established communion, the Church belongs to God and does not exist for itself. It is by its very nature missionary, called and sent to witness in its own life to that communion which God intends for all humanity and for all creation in the kingdom.

14. The Church is centred and grounded in the Gospel, the proclamation of the Incarnate Word, Jesus Christ, Son of the Father. This is reflected in the New Testament affirmation, "You have been born anew, not of perishable but of imperishable seed, through the living and enduring word of God" (1 Pet. 1:23). Through the preaching of the Gospel (cf. Rom. 10:14-18) and under the power of the Holy Spirit (cf. 1 Cor. 12:3), human beings come to saving faith and, by sacramental means, are incorporated into the body of Christ (cf. Eph. 1:23). Some communities, following this teaching, would call the Church *creatura evangelii* or "creature of the Gospel."[3] A defining aspect of the Church's life is

---

[2] This theme will be taken up in §§28-30 below.

[3] See the section "The Church as 'Creature of the Gospel'" in Lutheran-Roman Catholic Dialogue, "Church and Justification," in J. Gros, FSC, H. Meyer and W. G. Rusch, (eds.), *Growth in Agreement II: Reports and Agreed Statements of Ecumenical Conversations on a World Level, 1982-1998*, Geneva-Grand Rapids, WCC-Eerdmans, 2000, 495-498, which refers to Martin Luther's use of this expression in *WA* 2, 430, 6-7: "*Ecclesia enim creatura est evangelii.*" Some bilateral dialogues have used the Latin *creatura verbi* to express this same idea: see the section "Two Conceptions of the Church" (§§94-113), which describes the Church as *creatura verbi* and "sacrament of

to be a community that hears and proclaims the word of God. The Church draws life from the Gospel and discovers ever anew the direction for her journey.

15. The response of Mary, the Mother of God (*Theotokos*), to the angel's message at the annunciation, "Let it be done with me according to your word" (Luke 1:38), has been seen as a symbol of and model for the Church and the individual Christian. The Faith and Order study document *Church and World* (1990) noted that Mary is "an important example for all who seek to understand the full dimensions of life in Christian community" in that she receives and responds to the Word of God (Luke 1:26-38); shares the joy of the good news with Elizabeth (Luke 1:46-55); meditates, suffers and strives to understand the events of the birth and childhood of Jesus (Matt. 2:13-23; Luke 2:19, 41-51); seeks to comprehend the full implications of discipleship (Mark 3:31-35; Lk 18:19-20); stands by him under the cross and accompanies his body to the tomb (Matt. 27:55-61; John 19:25-27) and waits with the disciples and receives with them the Holy Spirit on Pentecost (Acts 1:12-14; 2:1-4).[4]

16. Christ prayed to the Father to send the Spirit on his disciples to guide them into all truth (John 15:26, 16:13), and it is the Spirit who not only bestows faith and other charisms upon individual believers but also equips the Church with its essential gifts, qualities and order. The Holy Spirit nourishes and enlivens the body of Christ through the living voice of the preached Gospel, through sacramental communion, especially in the Eucharist, and through ministries of service.

The Prophetic, Priestly and Royal People of God

17. In the call of Abraham, God was choosing for himself a holy people. The prophets frequently recalled this election and vocation in the following powerful formulation: "I will be their God, and they shall be my people" (Jer. 31:33; Ezek. 37:27; echoed in 2 Cor. 6:16; Heb. 8:10). The covenant with Israel marked a decisive moment in the unfolding realization of the plan of salvation. Christians believe that in the ministry, death and resurrection of Jesus and the sending of the Holy Spirit, God established the new covenant for the purpose of uniting all human beings with himself and with one another. There is a genuine newness in the covenant initiated by Christ and yet the Church remains, in God's design, profoundly related to the people of the first covenant, to whom God will always remain faithful (cf. Rom. 11:11-36).

18. In the Old Testament, the people of Israel are journeying towards the fulfilment of the promise that in Abraham all the nations of the earth shall be blessed. All those who turn to Christ find this promise fulfilled in him, when, on the cross, he broke down the dividing wall between Jew and Gentile (cf. Eph. 2:14). The Church is a "chosen race, a royal priesthood, a holy nation, God's own people" (1 Pet. 2:9-10). While acknowledging the unique priesthood of Jesus Christ, whose one sacrifice institutes the new covenant (cf. Heb. 9:15), believers are called to express by their lives the fact that they have been named a "royal priesthood," offering themselves "as a living sacrifice, holy and acceptable to God" (Rom. 12:1). Every Christian receives gifts of the Holy Spirit for the upbuilding of the Church and for his or

---

grace" in the Reformed-Roman Catholic Dialogue, "Towards a Common Understanding of the Church," in *Growth in Agreement II*, 801-805. See also the statement "Called to Be the One Church," cf. footnote 1, above.

[4] See the Faith and Order report *Church and World: The Unity of the Church and the Renewal of Human Community*, Geneva, WCC, 1990, 64. See also the report of the Anglican-Roman Catholic International Commission, "Mary: Grace and Hope in Christ," *Growth in Agreement III*, 82-112; and the report of the Groupe des Dombes, *Mary in the Plan of God and in the Communion of Saints* (1997-1998), Mahwah, N.J., Paulist Press, 2002.

her part in the mission of Christ. These gifts are given for the common good (cf. 1 Cor. 12:7; Eph. 4:11-13) and place obligations of responsibility and mutual accountability on every individual and local community and on the Church as a whole at every level of its life. Strengthened by the Spirit, Christians are called to live out their discipleship in a variety of forms of service.

19. The whole people of God is called to be a prophetic people, bearing witness to God's word; a priestly people, offering the sacrifice of a life lived in discipleship; and a royal people, serving as instruments for the establishment of God's reign. All members of the Church share in this vocation. In calling and sending the Twelve, Jesus laid foundations for the leadership of the community of his disciples in their ongoing proclamation of the kingdom. Faithful to his example, from the earliest times some believers were chosen under the guidance of the Spirit and given specific authority and responsibility. Ordained ministers "assemble and build up the Body of Christ by proclaiming and teaching the Word of God, by celebrating the sacraments and by guiding the life of the community in its worship, its mission and its caring ministry."[5] All members of the body, ordained and lay, are interrelated members of God's priestly people. Ordained ministers remind the community of its dependence on Jesus Christ, who is the source of its unity and mission, even as they understand their own ministry as dependent on him. At the same time, they can fulfill their calling only in and for the Church; they need its recognition, support and encouragement.

20. There is widespread agreement among churches of different traditions about the vital place of ministry. This was succinctly expressed in the Faith and Order document, *Baptism, Eucharist and Ministry* (1982), which stated that "the Church has never been without persons holding specific authority and responsibility," noting that, "Jesus chose and sent the disciples to be witnesses of the kingdom."[6] The mission which Jesus entrusted to the eleven in Matthew 28 entails "a ministry of word, sacrament and oversight given by Christ to the Church to be carried out by some of its members for the good of all. This triple function of the ministry equips the Church for its mission in the world."[7] Agreed statements are making it clear that the royal priesthood of the whole people of God (cf. 1 Pet. 2:9) and a special ordained ministry are both important aspects of the church, and not to be seen as mutually exclusive alternatives. At the same time, churches differ about who is competent to make final decisions for the community; for some that task is restricted to the ordained, while others see the laity as having a role in such decisions.

Body of Christ and Temple of the Holy Spirit

21. Christ is the abiding head of his body the Church, guiding, purifying and healing it (cf. Eph. 5:26). At the same time, he is intimately united to it, giving life to the whole in the Spirit (Rom. 12:5; cf. 1 Cor. 12:12). Faith in Christ is fundamental to membership of the body

---

[5] *Baptism, Eucharist and Ministry*, Geneva, WCC, 1982, section on Ministry, §13.

[6] Ibid., section on Ministry, §9.
[7] Reformed-Roman Catholic Dialogue, "Towards a Common Understanding of the Church", §132, in *Growth in Agreement II*, 810. See also the Lutheran-Roman Catholic report "Ministry in the Church," §17, in H. Meyer and L. Vischer (eds.), *Growth in Agreement: Reports and Agreed Statements of Ecumenical Conversations on a World Level*, Ramsey-Geneva, Paulist-WCC, 1984, 252-253: "The New Testament shows how there emerged from among the ministries a special ministry which was understood as standing in the succession of the apostles sent by Christ. Such a special ministry proved to be necessary for the sake of leadership in the communities. One can, therefore, say that according to the New Testament the 'special ministry' established by Jesus Christ through the calling and sending of the apostles 'was essential then – it is essential in all times and circumstances.'" The Methodist-Roman Catholic "Toward a Statement on the Church," affirms that "the church has always needed a God-given ministry," cf. *Growth in Agreement II*, 588, §29.

(Rom. 10:9). According to the understanding of most traditions, it is also through the rites or sacraments of initiation that human beings become members of Christ and in the Lord's Supper their participation in his body (cf. 1 Cor. 10:16) is renewed again and again. The Holy Spirit confers manifold gifts upon the members and brings forth their unity for the building up of the body (cf. Rom. 12:4-8; 1 Cor. 12:4-30). He renews their hearts, equipping and calling them to good works,[8] thus enabling them to serve the Lord in furthering the kingdom in the world. Thus the image of "body of Christ," though explicitly and primarily referring the Church to Christ, also deeply implies a relation to the Holy Spirit, as witnessed to throughout the entire New Testament. A vivid example of this is the account of the descent of tongues of fire upon the disciples gathered in the upper room on the morning of Pentecost (cf. Acts 2:1-4). By the power of the Holy Spirit believers grow into "a holy temple in the Lord" (Eph. 2:21-22), into a "spiritual house" (1 Pet. 2:5). Filled with the Holy Spirit, they are called to lead a life worthy of their calling in worship, witness and service, eager to maintain the unity of the Spirit in the bond of peace (cf. Eph. 4:1-3). The Holy Spirit enlivens and equips the Church to play its role in proclaiming and bringing about that general transformation for which all creation groans (cf. Rom. 8:22-23).

The One, Holy, Catholic and Apostolic Church

22. Since the time of the second ecumenical council, held at Constantinople in 381, most Christians have included in their liturgies the creed which professes the Church to be one, holy, catholic and apostolic. These attributes, which are not separate from one another but which inform one another and are mutually interrelated, are God's gifts to the Church which believers, in all their human frailty, are constantly called to actualize.

- The Church is one because God is one (cf. John 17:11; 1 Tim. 2:5). In consequence, the apostolic faith is one; the new life in Christ is one; the hope of the Church is one.[9] Jesus prayed that all his disciples be one so that the world might believe (cf. John 17:20-21) and sent the Spirit to form them into one body (cf. 1 Cor. 12:12-13). Current divisions within and between the churches stand in contrast to this oneness; "these must be overcome through the Spirit's gifts of faith, hope, and love so that separation and exclusion do not have the last word."[10] Yet, in spite of all divisions, all the churches understand themselves as founded in the one Gospel (cf. Gal. 1:5-9), and they are united in many features of their lives (cf. Eph. 4:4-7).

- The Church is holy because God is holy (cf. Is. 6:3; Lev. 11:44-45). Jesus "loved the Church and gave himself up for her in order to make her holy by cleansing her with the washing of water by the word...so that she may be holy and without blemish." (Eph. 5:25b-27). The essential holiness of the Church is witnessed to in every generation by holy men and women and by the holy words and actions the Church proclaims and performs in the name of God, the All Holy. Nevertheless, sin, which contradicts this holiness and runs counter to the Church's true nature and vocation, has again and again disfigured the lives of believers. For this reason,

---

[8] Cf. the Lutheran-Roman Catholic *Joint Declaration on the Doctrine of Justification*, Grand Rapids, Eerdmans, 2000, §15.

[9] Cf. "Called to Be the One Church," §5, in *Growth in Agreement III*, 607.
[10] Ibid.

part of the holiness of the Church is its ministry of continually calling people to repentance, renewal and reform.

- The Church is catholic because of the abundant goodness of God "who desires everyone to be saved and come to the knowledge of the truth" (1 Tim. 2:4). Through the life-giving power of God, the Church's mission transcends all barriers and proclaims the Gospel to all peoples. Where the whole mystery of Christ is present, there too is the Church catholic (cf. Ignatius of Antioch, *Letter to the Smyrneans*, 6), as in the celebration of the eucharist. The essential catholicity of the Church is undermined when cultural and other differences are allowed to develop into division. Christians are called to remove all obstacles to the embodiment of this fullness of truth and life bestowed upon the Church by the power of the Holy Spirit.

- The Church is apostolic because the Father sent the Son to establish it. The Son, in turn, chose and sent the apostles and prophets, empowered with the gifts of the Holy Spirit at Pentecost, to serve as its foundation and to oversee its mission (cf. Eph. 2:20; Rev. 21:14; and Clement of Rome, *Letter to the Corinthians* 42). The Christian community is called to be ever faithful to these apostolic origins; infidelity in worship, witness or service contradicts the Church's apostolicity. Apostolic succession in ministry, under the guidance of the Holy Spirit, is intended to serve the apostolicity of the Church.[11]

---

[11] The World Council of Churches statement "Called to Be the One Church," §3-7, offers a similar explanation of the creed's profession that the Church is "one, holy, catholic and apostolic." Cf. *Growth in Agreement III*, 607.

23. In the light of the previous paragraphs (13-22), it is clear that the Church is not merely the sum of individual believers among themselves. The Church is fundamentally a communion in the Triune God and, at the same time, a communion whose members partake together in the life and mission of God (cf. 2 Pet. 1:4), who, as Trinity, is the source and focus of all communion. Thus the Church is both a divine and a human reality.

24. While it is a common affirmation that the Church is a meeting place between the divine and the human, churches nonetheless have different sensitivities or even contrasting convictions concerning the way in which the Holy Spirit's activity in the Church is related to institutional structures or ministerial order. Some see certain essential aspects of the Church's order as willed and instituted by Christ himself for all time; therefore, in faithfulness to the Gospel, Christians would have no authority fundamentally to alter this divinely instituted structure. Some affirm that the ordering of the Church according to God's calling can take more than one form while others affirm that no single institutional order can be attributed to the will of God. Some hold that faithfulness to the Gospel may at times require a break in institutional continuity, while others insist that such faithfulness can be maintained by resolving difficulties without breaks which lead to separation.

How continuity and change in the Church relate to God's will

Through their patient encounter, in a spirit of mutual respect and attention, many churches have come to a deeper understanding of these differing sensitivities and convictions regarding continuity and change in the Church. In that deeper understanding, it becomes clear that the same intent — to obey God's will for the ordering of the Church — may, in some, inspire commitment to continuity and, in others, commitment to change. We invite the churches to recognize and honour each other's commitment to seeking the will of God in the ordering of the Church. We further invite them to reflect together about the criteria which are employed in different churches for considering issues about continuity and change. How far are such criteria open to development in the light of the urgent call of Christ to reconciliation (cf. Matt. 5:23-24)? Could this be the time for a new approach?

C. The Church as Sign and Servant of God's Design for the World

25. It is God's design to gather humanity and all of creation into communion under the Lordship of Christ (cf. Eph. 1:10). The Church, as a reflection of the communion of the Triune God, is meant to serve this goal and is called to manifest God's mercy to human beings, helping them to achieve the purpose for which they were created and in which their joy ultimately is found: to praise and glorify God together with all the heavenly hosts. This mission of the Church is fulfilled by its members through the witness of their lives and, when possible, through the open proclamation of the good news of Jesus Christ. The mission of the Church is to serve this purpose. Since God wills all people to be saved and to come to the knowledge of the truth (cf. 1 Tim. 2:4), Christians acknowledge that God reaches out to those who are not explicit members of the Church, in ways that may not be immediately evident to human eyes. While respecting the elements of truth and goodness that can be found in other religions and among those with no religion, the mission of the Church remains that of inviting, through witness and testimony, all men and women to come to know and love Christ Jesus.

26. Some New Testament passages use the term *mystery* (*mysterion*) to speak both of God's design of salvation in Christ (cf. Eph. 1:9; 3:4-6) and of the intimate relation between Christ and the Church (cf. Eph. 5:32; Col. 1:24-28). This suggests that the Church enjoys a spiritual, transcendent quality which cannot be grasped simply by looking at its visible appearance. The earthly and spiritual dimensions of the Church cannot be separated. The organizational structures of the Christian community need to be seen and evaluated, for good or ill, in the light of God's gifts of salvation in Christ, celebrated in the liturgy. The Church, embodying in its own life the mystery of salvation and the transfiguration of humanity, participates in the mission of Christ to reconcile all things to God and to one another through Christ (cf. 2 Cor. 5:18-21; Rom. 8:18-25).

27. While there is wide agreement that God established the Church as the privileged means for bringing about his universal design of salvation, some communities believe that this can be suitably expressed by speaking of the "Church as sacrament," while others do not normally use such language or reject it outright. Those who use the expression "Church as sacrament" do so because they understand the Church as an effective sign and means (sometimes described by the word *instrument*) of the communion of human beings with one another through their communion in the Triune God.[12] Those who refrain from employing

---

[12] For example, the Catholic bishops at the Second Vatican Council stated that "the Church, in Christ, is in the nature of sacrament – a sign and instrument, that is, of communion with God and of unity among all men" (cf. the Dogmatic Constitution on the Church, *Lumen Gentium*, n. 1), where the word *instrument* is intended to convey in a positive way the "effectiveness" of the Church. Other Christians who strongly affirm the Church's sacramental nature find inappropriate the use of the word *instrument* in reference to the Christian community. The rather wide reception of the idea that the Church is a sign is witnessed in the World Council of Churches report "The Holy

this expression believe that its use could obscure the distinction between the Church as a whole and the individual sacraments and that it may lead one to overlook the sinfulness still present among members of the community. All agree that God is the author of salvation; differences appear concerning the ways in which the various communities understand the nature and role of the Church and its rites in that saving activity.

The expression, "the Church as sacrament"

Those who use the expression "the Church as sacrament" do not deny the unique "sacramentality" of the sacraments nor do they deny the frailty of human ministers. Those who reject this expression, on the other hand, do not deny that the Church is an effective sign of God's presence and action. Might this, therefore, be seen as a question where legitimate differences of formulation are compatible and mutually acceptable?

D. Communion in Unity and Diversity

28. Legitimate diversity in the life of communion is a gift from the Lord. The Holy Spirit bestows a variety of complementary gifts on the faithful for the common good (cf. 1 Cor. 12:4-7). The disciples are called to be fully united (cf. Acts 2:44-47; 4:32-37), while respectful of and enriched by their diversities (1 Cor 12:14-26). Cultural and historical factors contribute to the rich diversity within the Church. The Gospel needs to be proclaimed in languages, symbols and images that are relevant to particular times and contexts so as to be lived authentically in each time and place. Legitimate diversity is compromised whenever Christians consider their own cultural expressions of the Gospel as the only authentic ones, to be imposed upon Christians of other cultures.

29. At the same time, unity must not be surrendered. Through shared faith in Christ, expressed in the proclamation of the Word, the celebration of the sacraments, and lives of service and witness, each local church is in communion with the local churches of all places and all times. A pastoral ministry for the service of unity and the upholding of diversity is one of the important means given to the Church in aiding those with different gifts and perspectives to remain mutually accountable to each other.

30. Issues concerning unity and diversity have been a principal concern since the Church discerned, with the aid of the Holy Spirit, that Gentiles were to be welcomed into communion (cf. Acts 15:1-29; 10:1-11:18). The letter addressed from the meeting in Jerusalem to the Christians in Antioch contains what might be called a fundamental principle governing unity and diversity: "For it has seemed good to the Holy Spirit and to us to impose on you no further burden than these essentials" (Acts 15:28). Later, the Ecumenical Councils provided further examples of such "essentials," as when, at the first Ecumenical Council (Nicaea, 325), the bishops clearly taught that communion in faith required the affirmation of the divinity of Christ. In more recent times, churches have joined together in enunciating firm ecclesial teachings which express the implications of such foundational doctrine, as in the condemnation of apartheid by many Christian communities.[13] There

---

Spirit and the Catholicity of the Church" from the Fourth General Assembly of the WCC held at Uppsala in 1968, which stated: "The Church is bold in speaking of itself as the sign of the coming unity of mankind." Cf. N. Goodall (ed.), *The Uppsala Report*, Geneva, WCC, 1968, 17. For the Dogmatic Constitution *Lumen Gentium* see http://www.vatican.va.

[13] "World Council of Churches' Consultation with Member-Churches in South Africa - Cottesloe, Johannesburg, 7-14 December, 1960," in *The Ecumenical Review*, XIII(2), January 1961, 244-250; "Statement on Confessional Integrity," in *In Christ a New Community: The Proceedings of the*

are limits to legitimate diversity; when it goes beyond acceptable limits it can be destructive of the gift of unity. Within the Church, heresies and schisms, along with political conflicts and expressions of hatred, have threatened God's gift of communion. Christians are called not only to work untiringly to overcome divisions and heresies but also to preserve and treasure their legitimate differences of liturgy, custom and law and to foster legitimate diversities of spirituality, theological method and formulation in such a way that they contribute to the unity and catholicity of the Church as a whole.[14]

Sixth Assembly of the Lutheran World Federation: Dar-es-Salaam, Tanzania, June 13-25, 1977, Geneva, Lutheran World Federation, 1977. 179-180, 210-212; "Resolution on Racism and South Africa," in *Ottawa 82: Proceedings of the 21st General Council of the World Alliance of Reformed Churches (Presbyterian and Congregational) Held at Ottawa, Canada, August 17-27, 1982*, Geneva, Offices of the Alliance, 1983, 176-180; The Belhar Confession, http://www.urcsa.org.za/documents/The%20Belhar%20Confession.pdf.

[14] Cf. the World Council of Churches statement "The Unity of the Church as *Koinonia*: Gift and Calling": "Diversities which are rooted in theological traditions, various cultural, ethnic or historical contacts are integral to the nature of communion; yet there are limits to diversity. Diversity is illegitimate when, for instance, it makes impossible the common confession of Jesus Christ as God and Saviour the same yesterday, today and forever (Heb. 13:8).... In communion diversities are brought together in harmony as gifts of the Holy Spirit, contributing to the richness and fullness of the church of God." In M. Kinnamon (ed.), *Signs of the Spirit: Official Report Seventh Assembly*, Geneva-Grand Rapids, WCC-Eerdmans, 1991, 173. Legitimate diversity is frequently treated in the international bilateral dialogues. The Anglican-Orthodox dialogue, for instance, notes the wide diversity in life of the local churches: "As long as their witness to the one faith remains unimpaired, such diversity is seen not as a deficiency or cause for division, but as a mark of the fullness of the one Spirit who distributes to each according to his will." *The Church of the Triune God: The Cyprus Statement Agreed by the International Commission for Anglican-Orthodox Dialogue 2006*, London, Anglican Communion Office, 2006, 91. See also: Lutheran-Roman Catholic Dialogue, *Facing Unity*, 1984, §§5-7, 27-30, and especially 31-34, in *Growth in Agreement II* 445-446, 449-450; Anglican-Roman Catholic International Commission, *The Gift of Authority*, §§26-31, in *Growth in Agreement III*, 68-69; Methodist-Roman Catholic Dialogue, *Speaking the Truth in Love*, §50, in *Growth in Agreement III*, 154.

Legitimate and divisive diversity

Ecumenical dialogue in search of the unity for which Christ prayed has, in large part, been an effort by representatives from various Christian churches to discern, with the help of the Holy Spirit, what is necessary for unity, according to the will of God, and what is properly understood as legitimate diversity. Though all churches have their own procedures for distinguishing legitimate from illegitimate diversity, it is clear that two things are lacking: (a) common criteria, or means of discernment, and (b) such mutually recognized structures as are needed to use these effectively. All churches seek to follow the will of the Lord yet they continue to disagree on some aspects of faith and order and, moreover, on whether such disagreements are Church-divisive or, instead, part of legitimate diversity. We invite the churches to consider: what positive steps can be taken to make common discernment possible?

E. Communion of Local Churches

31. The ecclesiology of communion provides a helpful framework for considering the relation between the local church and the universal Church. Most Christians could agree that the local church is "a community of baptized believers in which the word of God is preached, the apostolic faith confessed, the sacraments are celebrated, the redemptive work of Christ for the world is witnessed to, and a ministry of *episkopé* exercised by bishops or other ministers in serving the community."[15] Culture, language and shared history all enter into the very fabric of the local church. At the same time, the Christian community in each place shares with all the other local communities all that

---

[15] Cf. the report of the Joint Working Group of the World Council of Churches and the Roman Catholic Church, "The Church: Local and Universal," §15, in *Growth in Agreement II*, 866. "Local" should not be confused with "denominational" in this description.

is essential to the life of communion. Each local church contains within it the fullness of what it is to be the Church. It is wholly Church, but not the whole Church. Thus, the local church should not be seen in isolation from but in dynamic relation with other local churches. From the beginning communion was maintained between local churches by collections, exchanges of letters, visits, eucharistic hospitality and tangible expressions of solidarity (cf. 1 Cor. 16; 2 Cor. 8:1-9; Gal. 2:1-10). From time to time, during the first centuries, local churches assembled to take counsel together. All of these were ways of nurturing interdependence and maintaining communion. This communion of local churches is thus not an optional extra. The universal Church is the communion of all local churches united in faith and worship around the world.[16] It is not merely the sum, federation or juxtaposition of local churches, but all of them together are the same Church present and acting in this world. Catholicity, as described in the baptismal catechesis of Cyril of Jerusalem, refers not simply to geographic extension but also to the manifold variety of local churches and their participation in the fullness of faith and life that unites them in the one *koinonia*.[17]

32. Within this shared understanding of the communion of the local churches in the universal Church, differences arise, not only about the geographical extent of the community intended by the expression "local church" but also in relation to the role of bishops.

Some churches are convinced that the bishop, as a successor to the apostles, is essential to the structure and reality of the local church. Thus, in a strict sense, the local church is a diocese, comprised of a number of parishes. For others, having developed various forms of self-understanding, the expression "local church" is less common and not defined in reference to the ministry of a bishop. For some of those churches, the local church is simply the congregation of believers gathered in one place to hear the Word and celebrate the Sacraments. Both for those who see the bishop as essential and for those who do not, the expression "local church" has also at times been used to refer to a regional configuration of churches, gathered together in a synodal structure under a presidency. Finally there is not yet agreement about how local, regional and universal levels of ecclesial order relate to one another, although valuable steps in seeking convergence about those relations can be found in both multilateral and bilateral dialogues.[18]

The relationship between local and universal Church

Many churches can embrace a shared understanding of the fundamental relationship and communion of local churches within the universal Church. They share the understanding that the presence of Christ, by the will of the Father and the power of the Spirit, is truly manifested in the local church (it is "wholly Church"), and that this very presence

---

[16] Cf. the unity statements of the New Delhi, Uppsala, and Nairobi assemblies of the World Council of Churches in W. A. Visser 't Hooft (ed.), *The New Delhi Report: The Third Assembly of the World Council of Churches 1961*, London, SCM, 1962, 116-134; N. Goodall (ed.), *The Uppsala Report 1968: Official Report of the Fourth Assembly of the World Council of Churches*, Geneva, WCC, 1968, 11-19; and D. M. Paton (ed.), *Breaking Barriers Nairobi 1975: The Official Report of the Fifth Assembly of the World Council of Churches*, London-Grand Rapids, SPCK-Eerdmans, 1976, 59-69.

[17] Cyril of Jerusalem, *Catechesis 18*, in J. P. Migne, *Patrologia Graeca* 33, 1044.

[18] A good example at the multilateral level is the report of the Joint Working Group of the World Council of Churches and the Roman Catholic Church "The Church: Local and Universal," in http://www.oikoumene.org/en/resources/documents/wcc-commissions/. Cf. also *Growth in Agreement II*, 862-875. From the bilateral dialogues, see "Ecclesial Communion – Communion of Churches" of the Lutheran-Roman Catholic "Church and Justification," in *Growth in Agreement II*, 505-512; and especially the Orthodox-Roman Catholic statement on "Ecclesiological and Canonical Consequences of the Sacramental Nature of the Church: Ecclesial Communion, Conciliarity and Authority" (2007) at: http://www.pcf.va/romancuria/pontifical_councils/chrstuni/ch_orthodox_docs/re_pc_chrstuni_doc_20071013_documento-ravenna_en.html.

of Christ impels the local church to be in communion with the universal Church (it is not "the whole Church"). Where this fundamental agreement is found, the expression "local church" may nonetheless be used in varying ways. In our common quest for closer unity, we invite the churches to seek more precise mutual understanding and agreement in this area: what is the appropriate relation between the various levels of life of a fully united Church and what specific ministries of leadership are needed to serve and foster those relations?

CHAPTER III
The Church: Growing in Communion

A. Already but Not Yet

33. The Church is an eschatological reality, already anticipating the kingdom, but not yet its full realization. The Holy Spirit is the principal agent in establishing the kingdom and in guiding the Church so that it can be a servant of God's work in this process. Only as we view the present in the light of the activity of the Holy Spirit, guiding the whole process of salvation history to its final recapitulation in Christ to the glory of the Father, do we begin to grasp something of the mystery of the Church.

34. On the one hand, as the communion of believers held in personal relationship with God, the Church is already the eschatological community God wills. Visible and tangible signs which express that this new life of communion has been effectively realized are: receiving and sharing the faith of the apostles, baptising, breaking and sharing the eucharistic bread, praying with and for one another and for the needs of the world, serving one another in love, participating in each other's joys and sorrows, giving material aid, proclaiming and witnessing to the good news in mission and working together for justice and peace. On the other hand, as an historical reality the Church is made up of human beings who are subject to the conditions of the world. One such condition is change,[1] either positive in the sense of growth and development or negative in the sense of decline and distortion. Other conditions include cultural

---

[1] This condition of change is not meant to obscure the enduring meaning of Jesus Christ and his Gospel: "Jesus Christ is the same yesterday and today and forever" (Heb. 13:8).

and historical factors which can have either a positive or a negative impact on the Church's faith, life and witness.

35. As a pilgrim community the Church contends with the reality of sin. Ecumenical dialogue has shown that there are deep, commonly-held convictions behind what have sometimes been seen as conflicting views concerning the relation between the Church's holiness and human sin. There are significant differences in the way in which Christians articulate these common convictions. For some, their tradition affirms that the Church is sinless since, being the body of the sinless Christ, it cannot sin. Others consider that it is appropriate to refer to the Church as sinning, since sin may become systemic so as to affect the institution of the Church itself and, although sin is in contradiction to the true identity of the Church, it is nonetheless real. The different ways in which various communities understand sin itself, whether primarily as moral imperfection or primarily as a break in relationship, as well as whether and how sin may be systemic, can also have an impact upon this question.

36. The Church is the body of Christ; according to his promise, the gates of hell cannot prevail against it (cf. Matt. 16:18). Christ's victory over sin is complete and irreversible, and by Christ's promise and grace Christians have confidence that the Church will always share in the fruits of that victory. They also share the realization that, in this present age, believers are vulnerable to the power of sin, both individually and collectively. All churches acknowledge the fact of sin among believers and its often grievous impact. All recognize the continual need for Christian self-examination, penitence, conversion (*metanoia*), reconciliation and renewal. Holiness and sin relate to the life of the Church in different and unequal ways. Holiness expresses the Church's identity according to the will of God, while sin stands in contradiction to this identity (cf. Rom. 6:1-11).

B. Growing in the Essential Elements of Communion: Faith, Sacraments, Ministry

37. The journey towards the full realization of God's gift of communion requires Christian communities to agree about the fundamental aspects of the life of the Church. "The ecclesial elements required for full communion within a visibly united church – the goal of the ecumenical movement – are communion in the fullness of apostolic faith; in sacramental life; in a truly one and mutually recognized ministry; in structures of conciliar relations and decision-making; and in common witness and service in the world."[2] These attributes serve as a necessary framework for maintaining unity in legitimate diversity. Moreover, the growth of churches towards the unity of the one Church is intimately related to their calling to promote the unity of the whole of

[2] From "The Church: Local and Universal," 1990, §25, in *Growth in Agreement II*, 868. Paragraphs 10-11 and 28-32 of this text demonstrate with quotations and footnotes the fact that its presentation of communion has been drawn from a wide range of ecumenical dialogues involving Anglicans, Lutherans, Methodists, Orthodox, Reformed and Roman Catholics, as well as several statements on unity adopted at some of the Assemblies of the WCC (cf. footnote 16, ch. 2). The World Council of Churches statement, "The Unity of the Church as *Koinonia*: Gift and Calling," enhances the ministerial element by adding the word *reconciled* to *recognized* [M. Kinnamon (ed.), *Signs of the Spirit: Official Report Seventh Assembly*, Geneva, WCC, 1991, 173]. Similar configurations of the fundamental components of communion appear in the Lutheran-Roman Catholic document "Facing Unity," in *Growth in Agreement II*, 456-477, which presents the church as a community of faith, sacraments and service; and the Methodist-Roman Catholic text "The Apostolic Tradition," in *Growth in Agreement II*, 610-613, which describes the living body of the church in terms of faith, worship and ministry. The classic unity statements from the WCC general assemblies of New Delhi (1960), Nairobi (1975), Canberra (1990) and Porto Alegre (2006) also present the essential qualities of unity, as the following quotation from the last of these may serve to illustrate: "Our churches have affirmed that the unity for which we pray, hope, and work is 'a *koinonia* given and expressed in the common confession of the apostolic faith; a common sacramental life entered by the one baptism and celebrated together in one eucharistic fellowship; a common life in which members and ministries are mutually recognized and reconciled; and a common mission witnessing to the gospel of God's grace to all people and serving the whole of creation.' Such *koinonia* is to be expressed in each place, and through a conciliar relationship of churches in different places," in "Called to Be the One Church," §2, *Growth in Agreement III*, 606-607.

humanity and of creation, since Christ, who is head of the Church, is the one in whom all are to be reconciled. Dialogue, such as that which accompanied the writing and reception of *Baptism, Eucharist and Ministry*, has already registered significant progress in convergence about these essential elements of communion, though less on ministry than on the other two. It is not the intention of the present text to repeat those past achievements but rather to summarize them briefly and to indicate a few of the further steps forward that have been made in recent years.

Faith

38. Regarding the first of these elements, there is widespread agreement that the Church is called to proclaim, in each generation, the faith "once for all entrusted to the saints" (Jude v. 3) and to remain steadfast in the teaching first handed on by the apostles. Faith is evoked by the Word of God, inspired by the grace of the Holy Spirit, attested in Scripture and transmitted through the living tradition of the Church. It is confessed in worship, life, service and mission. While it must be interpreted in the context of changing times and places, these interpretations must remain in continuity with the original witness and with its faithful explication throughout the ages. Faith has to be lived out in active response to the challenges of every age and place. It speaks to personal and social situations, including situations of injustice, of the violation of human dignity and of the degradation of creation.

39. Ecumenical dialogue has shown that, on many central aspects of Christian doctrine, there is a great deal that already unites believers.[3] In 1991, the study text

Confessing the One Faith not only succeeded in showing substantial agreement among Christians concerning the meaning of the Nicene Creed professed in the liturgies of most churches. It also explained how the faith of the creed is grounded in Scripture, confessed in the ecumenical symbol and has to be confessed afresh in relation to the challenges of the contemporary world. The intention was not only to help churches recognize fidelity to that faith in themselves and in others but also to provide a credible ecumenical tool for proclaiming the faith today. In 1998, *A Treasure in Earthen Vessels* explored the ongoing interpretation of Scripture and Tradition in handing on the faith, noting: "The Holy Spirit inspires and leads the churches each to rethink and reinterpret their tradition in conversation with each other, always aiming to embody the one Tradition in the unity of God's Church."[4] While the churches generally agree as to the importance of Tradition in the generation and subsequent interpretation of scripture, more recent dialogue has tried to understand how the Christian community engages in such interpretation. Many bilateral dialogues have acknowledged that ecclesial interpretation of the contemporary meaning of the Word of God involves the faith experience of the whole people, the insights of theologians, and the discernment of the ordained ministry.[5] The challenge

---

[3] See, for example, the chapters "Fundamentals of Our Common Faith: Jesus Christ and the Holy Trinity" and "Salvation, Justification, Sanctification" of Walter Kasper's, *Harvesting the Fruits: Basic Aspects of Christian Faith in Dialogue*,

London-New York, Continuum, 2009, 10-47, which recounts convergence about these topics among Anglicans, Lutherans, Methodists, Reformed and Roman Catholics.

[4] *A Treasure in Earthen Vessels*, Geneva, WCC, 1998, §32. Earlier, *Baptism, Eucharist and Ministry*, section on Ministry, §34, had noted: "Apostolic tradition in the Church means continuity in the permanent characteristics of the Church of the apostles: witness to the apostolic faith, proclamation and fresh interpretation of the Gospel, celebration of baptism and the eucharist, transmission of ministerial responsibilities, communion in prayer, love, joy and suffering, service to the sick and the needy, unity among the local Churches and sharing the gifts which the Lord has given to each"; in *Baptism, Eucharist, Ministry*, Geneva, WCC, 1982.

[5] See, for example, the Lutheran-Orthodox statement "Scripture and Tradition," in *Growth in Agreement II*, 224-225; the Methodist-Roman Catholic "The Word of Life," §§62-72, describing the "Agents of Discernment,"

today is for churches to agree on how these factors work together.

Sacraments

40. Regarding the sacraments, the churches registered a significant degree of approval with the way in which *Baptism, Eucharist and Ministry* (1982) described the meaning and celebration of baptism and eucharist.[6] That text also suggested avenues seeking further convergence on what remained the most significant unresolved issues: who may be baptized, the presence of Christ in the eucharist and the relation of the eucharist to Christ's sacrifice on the cross. At the same time, while briefly commenting on chrismation or confirmation, *Baptism, Eucharist and Ministry* did not address the other rites celebrated in many communities and considered by some as sacraments, nor was it designed to take into account the view of those communities who affirm that their vocation does not include the rites of baptism and the eucharist, while affirming that they share in the sacramental life of the Church.

41. The growing convergence among churches in their understanding of baptism may be summarized as follows.[7] Through Baptism with water in the name of the Triune God, the Father, the Son and the Holy Spirit, Christians are united with Christ and with each other in the Church of every time and place. Baptism is the introduction to and celebration of new life in Christ and of participation in his baptism, life, death and resurrection (cf. Matt. 3:13-17; Rom. 6:3-5). It is "the water of rebirth and renewal by the Holy Spirit" (Titus 3,5) incorporating believers into the body of Christ and enabling them to share in the kingdom of God and the life of the world to come (cf. Eph 2:6). Baptism involves confession of sin, conversion of heart, pardoning, cleansing and sanctification; it consecrates the believer as a member of "a chosen race, a royal priesthood, a holy nation" (1 Pet. 2:9). Baptism is thus a basic bond of unity. Some churches see the gift of the Holy Spirit as given in a special way through chrismation or confirmation, which is considered by them as one of the sacraments of initiation. The general agreement about baptism has led some who are involved in the ecumenical movement to call for the mutual recognition of baptism.[8]

42. There is a dynamic and profound relation between baptism and the eucharist. The communion into which the newly initiated Christian enters is brought to fuller expression and nourished in the eucharist, which reaffirms baptismal faith and gives grace for the faithful living out of the Christian calling. The progress in agreement about the eucharist registered in ecumenical dialogue may be summarized as follows.[9] The Lord's

in *Growth in Agreement I*, 632-634; the Anglican-Roman Catholic "Gift of Authority," in *Growth in Agreement III*, 60-81; the Disciples-Roman Catholic "Receiving and Handing on the Faith: The Mission and Responsibility of the Church," in *Growth in Agreement III*, 121-137; the Methodist-Roman Catholic "Speaking the Truth in Love: Teaching Authority among Catholics and Methodists," in *Growth in Agreement III*, 138-176; and the Reformed-Oriental Orthodox "Report" (2001), §§22-28, describing "Tradition and Holy Scripture" and "The Role of the Theologian in the Christian Community," in *Growth in Agreement III*, 43-44.

[6] Cf. *Baptism, Eucharist and Ministry, 1982-1990: Report on the Process and Responses*, Geneva, WCC, 1990, 39, 55-56.

[7] This paragraph recounts the material elaborated under the subtitle "II. The Meaning of Baptism," in *Baptism, Eucharist and Ministry*, Section on Baptism, §§2-7. Very similar affirmations from four international bilateral dialogues are found in "Common Understanding of Baptism" of W. Kasper, *Harvesting the Fruits*, 164-168, as well as in the Faith and Order study text entitled *One*

Baptism: Towards Mutual Recognition, Geneva, WCC, 2011.

[8] An example of such mutual recognition of baptism was that achieved by eleven of the sixteen member communities of the Council of Christian Churches in Germany on April 29, 2007, which is recounted at http://www.ekd.de/english/mutual_recognition_of_baptism.html.

[9] This summary draws upon "II. The Meaning of the Eucharist" in *Baptism, Eucharist and Ministry*, section on Eucharist, §§2-26. For varying degrees of convergence between Anglicans, Lutherans, Methodists, Reformed and Roman Catholics, see "The Eucharist," in Kasper, *Harvesting the Fruits*, 168-190.

Supper is the celebration in which, gathered around his table, Christians receive the body and blood of Christ. It is a proclamation of the Gospel, a glorification of the Father for everything accomplished in creation, redemption and sanctification (*doxologia*); a memorial of the death and resurrection of Christ Jesus and what was accomplished once for all on the Cross (*anamnesis*); and an invocation of the Holy Spirit to transform both the elements of bread and wine and the participants themselves (*epiclesis*). Intercession is made for the needs of the Church and the world, the communion of the faithful is again deepened as an anticipation and foretaste of the kingdom to come, impelling them to go out and share Christ's mission of inaugurating that kingdom even now. St Paul highlights the connection between the Lord's Supper and the very life of the Church (cf. 1 Cor. 10:16-17; 11:17-33).

43. Just as the confession of faith and baptism are inseparable from a life of service and witness, so too the eucharist demands reconciliation and sharing by all those who are brothers and sisters in the one family of God. "Christians are called in the eucharist to be in solidarity with the outcast and to become signs of the love of Christ who lived and sacrificed himself for all and now gives himself in the eucharist.... The eucharist brings into the present age a new reality which transforms Christians into the image of Christ and therefore makes them his effective witnesses."[10] The liturgical renewal among some churches may be seen in part as a reception of the convergences registered in ecumenical dialogue about the sacraments.

44. Different Christian traditions have diverged as to whether baptism, eucharist and other rites should be termed "sacraments" or "ordinances." The word *sacrament* (used to translate the Greek *mysterion*) indicates that God's saving work is communicated in the action of the rite, whilst the term *ordinance* emphasizes that the action of the rite is performed in obedience to Christ's word and example.[11] These two positions have often been seen as mutually opposed. However, as the Faith and Order study text *One Baptism* points out, "Most traditions, whether they use the term 'sacrament' or 'ordinance', affirm that these events are both *instrumental* (in that God uses them to bring about a new reality), and *expressive* (of an already-existing reality). Some traditions emphasize the instrumental dimension.... Others emphasize the expressive dimension."[12] Might this difference then be more one of emphasis than of doctrinal disagreement? These rites express both the "institutional" and "charismatic" aspects of the Church. They are visible, effective actions instituted by Christ and, at the same time, are made effective by the action of the Holy Spirit who, by means of them, equips those who receive the sacraments with a variety of gifts for the edification of the Church and its mission in and for the world.

Sacraments and ordinances

In the light of the convergences on Baptism and Eucharist and of further reflection upon the historical roots and potential compatibility of the expressions "sacrament" and "ordinance," the churches are challenged to explore whether they are able to arrive at deeper agreement about that dimension of the life of the Church that involves these rites. Such convergence could lead them to consider several additional questions. Most churches celebrate other rites or sacraments, such as chrismations/confirmations, weddings and ordinations within their liturgies and many also have rites for the forgiveness of sin and the blessing of the sick:

---

[10] From *Baptism, Eucharist and Ministry,* section on "Ministry," §§24 and 26.

[11] The Latin term *sacramentum* denoted the oath that a recruit pronounced upon entering military service and was used by the first major theologian to write in the Latin language, Tertullian (160-220), in reference to baptism.
[12] *One Baptism: Towards Mutual Recognition*, §30.

may not the number and ecclesial status of these sacraments or ordinances be addressed in ecumenical dialogues? We also invite churches to consider whether they can now achieve closer convergence about who may receive baptism and who may preside at the Church's liturgical celebrations? Further, are there ways in which fuller mutual understanding can be established between the churches which celebrate these rites and those Christian communities convinced that the sharing of life in Christ does not require the celebration of sacraments or other rites?

Ministry within the Church

Ordained ministry

45. All churches affirm the biblical teaching that, unlike the many priests of the Old Covenant (cf. Heb. 7:23), Jesus, our high priest (cf. Heb. 8:10), offered his redeeming sacrifice "once for all" (cf. Heb. 7:27; 9:12; 9:26; 10:10, 12-14). They differ on the implications they draw from these texts. *Baptism, Eucharist and Ministry* noted that ordained ministers "may appropriately be called priests because they fulfil a particular priestly service by strengthening and building up the royal and prophetic priesthood of the faithful through word and sacraments, through their prayers of intercession, and through their pastoral guidance of the community."[13] In line with that view, some churches hold that ordained ministry stands in a special relationship with the unique priesthood of Christ that it is distinct from, even if related to, that royal priesthood described in 1 Pet. 2:9. These churches believe that some persons are ordained to a particular priestly function through the sacrament of ordination.[14] Others do not consider ordained ministers as "priests," nor do some understand ordination in

sacramental terms. Christians disagree as well over the traditional restriction of ordination to the ministry of word and sacrament to men only.

Ordained ministry

Ecumenical dialogue has repeatedly shown that issues relating to ordained ministry constitute challenging obstacles on the path to unity. If differences such as those relating to the priesthood of the ordained prohibit full unity, it must continue to be an urgent priority for the churches to discover how they can be overcome.

46. There is no single pattern of ministry in the New Testament, though all churches would look to Scripture in seeking to follow the will of the Lord concerning how ordained ministry is to be understood, ordered and exercised. At times, the Spirit has guided the Church to adapt its ministries to contextual needs (cf. Acts 6:1-6). Various forms of ministry have been blessed with the gifts of the Spirit. Early writers, such as Ignatius of Antioch, insisted upon the threefold ministry of bishop, presbyter and deacon.[15] This pattern of three related ministries can be seen to have roots in the New Testament; eventually it became the generally accepted pattern and is still considered normative by many churches today. Some churches, since the time of the Reformation, have adopted different patterns of ministry.[16] Among the several means for maintaining the Church's apostolicity, such as the scriptural canon, dogma and liturgical order, ordained ministry has played an important role. Succession in ministry is meant to serve the apostolic continuity of the Church.

---

[13] *Baptism, Eucharist and Ministry,* section on Ministry, §17.
[14] See Anglican-Roman Catholic "Ministry and Ordination" and "Elucidation," in *Growth in Agreement I*, 78-87; and Orthodox-Roman Catholic Dialogue, "The Sacrament of Order in the Sacramental Structure of the Church," in *Growth in Agreement II*, 671-679.

[15] Cf. Ignatius of Antioch's *Letter to the Magnesians* 6 and 13; *Letter to the Trallians* 7; *Letter to the Philadelphians* 4; *Letter to the Smyrnaeans* 8.
[16] Two insightful accounts of these Reformation developments are the Reformed-Roman Catholic text "Towards a Common Understanding of the Church," §§12-63, entitled "Toward a Reconciliation of Memories," in *Growth in Agreement II*, 781-795; and the Lutheran-Roman Catholic text, *The Apostolicity of the Church*, Minneapolis 2006, §§65-164, pages 40-71.

47. Almost all Christian communities today have a formal structure of ministry. Frequently this structure is diversified and reflects, more or less explicitly, the threefold pattern of *episkopos-presbyteros-diakonos*. Churches remain divided, however, as to whether or not the "historic episcopate" (meaning bishops ordained in apostolic succession back to the earliest generations of the Church), or the apostolic succession of ordained ministry more generally, is something intended by Christ for his community. Some believe that the threefold ministry of bishop, presbyter and deacon is a sign of continuing faithfulness to the Gospel and is vital to the apostolic continuity of the Church as a whole.[17] In contrast, others do not view faithfulness to the Gospel as closely bound to succession in ministry, and some are wary of the historic episcopate because they see it as vulnerable to abuse and thus potentially harmful to the well-being of the community. *Baptism, Eucharist and Ministry*, for its part, only affirmed that the threefold ministry "may serve today as an expression of the unity we seek and also as a means for achieving it."[18]

The threefold ministry

Given the signs of growing agreement about the place of ordained ministry in the Church, we are led to ask if the churches can achieve a consensus as to whether or not the threefold ministry is part of God's will for the Church in its realization of the unity which God wills.

The Gift of Authority in the Ministry of the Church

48. All authority in the Church comes from her Lord and head, Jesus Christ, whose authority, conveyed with the word *exousia* (power, delegated authority, moral authority, influence; literally "from out of one's being") in the New Testament, was exercised in his teaching (cf. Matt. 5:2; Luke 5:3), his performing of miracles (cf. Mark. 1:30-34; Matt. 14:35-36), his exorcisms (cf. Mark 1:27; Luke 4:35-36), his forgiveness of sins (cf. Mark 2:10; Luke 5:4) and his leading the disciples in the ways of salvation (cf. Matt. 16:24). Jesus' entire ministry was characterized by authority which placed itself at the service of human beings (Mark 1:27; Luke 4:36). Having received "all authority in heaven and on earth" (Matt. 28:18), Jesus shared his authority with the apostles (cf. John 20:22). Their successors in the ministry of oversight (*episkopé*) exercised authority in the proclamation of the Gospel, in the celebration of the sacraments, particularly the eucharist, and in the pastoral guidance of believers.[19]

49. The distinctive nature of authority in the Church can be understood and exercised correctly only in the light of the authority of its head, the one who was crucified, who "emptied himself" and "obediently accepted even death, death on the cross" (Phil. 2:7-8). This authority is to be understood within Jesus' eschatological promise to guide the Church to fulfillment in the reign of heaven. Thus, the Church's authority is

---

[17] On this point, the Lutheran-Roman Catholic "Church and Justification" (1993), §185, states: "There is no contradiction between the doctrine of justification and the idea of an ordained ministry instituted by God and necessary for the church" (*Growth in Agreement II*, 529). Nevertheless, a few paragraphs later, the same text adds: "The difference between the Catholic and the Lutheran views on the theological and ecclesiological evaluation of the episcopate is thus not so radical that a Lutheran rejection or even indifference towards this ministry stands in opposition to the Catholic assertion of its ecclesial indispensability. The question is rather one of a clear gradation in the evaluation of this ministry, which can be and has been described on the Catholic side by predicates such as 'necessary' or 'indispensable', and on the Lutheran side as 'important', 'meaningful' and thus 'desirable'" (§197; *(Growth in Agreement II*, 532).

[18] *Baptism, Eucharist and Ministry*, section on Ministry, §22.

[19] This basic description of the authority of Jesus and its sharing with the Church closely paraphrases the description offered by the Orthodox-Roman Catholic Ravenna Statement (2007) concerning "Ecclesiological and Canonical Consequences of the Sacramental Nature of the Church: Ecclesial Communion, Conciliarity and Authority," §12; see above, ch. II, n.18.

different from that of the world. When the disciples sought to exercise power over one another, Jesus corrected them, saying that he came not to be served but to serve, and to offer his life for others (cf. Mark 10:41-45; Luke 22:25). Authority within the Church must be understood as humble service, nourishing and building up the *koinonia* of the Church in faith, life and witness; it is exemplified in Jesus' action of washing the feet of the disciples (cf. John 13:1-17). It is a service (*diakonia*) of love, without any domination or coercion.

50. Thus, authority in the Church in its various forms and levels, must be distinguished from mere power. This authority comes from God the Father through the Son in the power of the Holy Spirit; as such it reflects the holiness of God. The sources of authority recognized in varying degrees by the churches such as Scripture, Tradition, worship, councils and synods, also reflect the holiness of the Triune God. Such authority is recognized wherever the truth which leads to holiness is expressed and the holiness of God is voiced "from the lips of children and infants" (Ps. 8:2; cf Matt. 21:16). Holiness means a greater authenticity in relationship with God, with others and with all creation. Throughout history the Church has recognized a certain authority in the lives of the saints, in the witness of monasticism and in various ways that groups of believers have lived out and expressed the truth of the gospel. Accordingly, a certain kind of authority may be recognized in the ecumenical dialogues and the agreed statements they produce, when they reflect a common search for and discovery of the truth in love (cf. Eph. 4:15), urge believers to seek the Lord's will for ecclesial communion, and invite ongoing *metanoia* and holiness of life.

51. The authority which Jesus Christ, the one head of the Church, shares with those in ministries of leadership is neither only personal, nor only delegated by the community. It is a gift of the Holy Spirit destined for the service (*diakonia*) of the Church in love. Its exercise includes the participation of the whole community, whose sense of the faith (*sensus fidei*) contributes to the overall understanding of God's Word and whose reception of the guidance and teaching of the ordained ministers testifies to the authenticity of that leadership. A relation of mutual love and dialogue unites those who exercise authority and those who are subject to it. As a means of guiding the Christian community in faith, worship and service with the *exousia* of the crucified and risen Lord, the exercise of authority can call for obedience, but such a call is meant to be welcomed with voluntary cooperation and consent since its aim is to assist believers in growing to full maturity in Christ (cf. Eph. 4:11-16).[20] The "sense" for the authentic meaning of the Gospel that is shared by the whole people of God, the insights of those dedicated in a special way to biblical and theological studies, and the guidance of those especially consecrated for the ministry of oversight, all collaborate in the discernment of God's will for the community. Decision-making in the Church seeks and elicits the consensus of all and depends upon the guidance of the Holy Spirit, discerned in attentive listening to God's Word and to one another. By the process of active reception over time, the Spirit resolves possible ambiguities in decisions. The ecumenical movement has made it possible for authoritative teaching by some Christian leaders to have an effect beyond the boundaries of their own communities, even now in our current state of division. For example, Archbishop Desmond Tutu's leadership in declaring that "apartheid was too strong to be overcome by a divided

---

[20] Cf. "Ecclesiological and Canonical Consequences of the Sacramental Nature of the Church: Ecclesial Communion, Conciliarity and Authority," §§13-14; see above ch. II, n.18.

Church,"[21] the initiatives by the Ecumenical Patriarch Bartholomew to unite Christian leaders in the cause of ecology, the efforts by Popes John Paul II and Benedict XVI to invite Christians and leaders from other faiths to join together in praying for and promoting peace, and of the influence of Brother Roger Schutz as he inspired countless Christian believers, especially the young, to join together in common worship of the Triune God.

Authority in the Church and its exercise

Significant steps towards convergence on authority and its exercise have been recorded in various bilateral dialogues.[22] *Differences continue to exist between churches, however, as to the relative weight to be accorded to the different sources of authority, as to how far and in what ways the Church has the means to arrive at a normative expression of its faith, and as to the role of ordained ministers in providing an authoritative interpretation of revelation. Yet all churches share the urgent concern that the Gospel be preached, interpreted and lived out in the world humbly, but with compelling authority. May not the seeking of ecumenical convergence on the way in which authority is recognized and exercised play a creative role in this missionary endeavour of the churches?*

The Ministry of Oversight (Episkopé)

52. The Church, as the body of Christ and the eschatological people of God, is built up by the Holy Spirit through a diversity of gifts or ministries. This diversity calls for a ministry of co-ordination so that these gifts may enrich the whole Church, its unity and mission.[23] The faithful exercise of the ministry of *episkopé* under the Gospel by persons chosen and set aside for such ministry is a requirement of fundamental importance for the Church's life and mission. The specific development of structures of *episkopé* varied in different times and places; but all communities, whether episcopally ordered or not, continued to see the need for a ministry of *episkopé*. In every case *episkopé* is in the service of maintaining continuity in apostolic faith and unity of life. In addition to preaching the Word and celebrating the Sacraments, a principal purpose of this ministry is faithfully to safeguard and hand on revealed truth, to hold the local congregations in communion, to give mutual support and to lead in witnessing to the Gospel. Such guidance includes the oversight of the various Christian service organizations dedicated to bettering human life and to the relief of suffering, aspects of the Church's service (*diakonia*) to the world to which we will return in the next chapter. All these functions, summed up in the term *episkopé* or oversight, are exercised by persons who relate to the faithful of their own communities as well as to those who exercise such a ministry in other local communities. This is what it means to affirm that the ministry of oversight, as all ministry in the Church, needs to be exercised in personal, collegial and communal ways.[24] These ways of exercise have been succinctly described in *Baptism,*

---

[21] Desmond Tutu, "Towards *Koinonia* in Faith, Life and Witness," in T. Best and G. Gassmann (eds.), *On the Way to Fuller Koinonia*, Geneva, WCC, 1994, 96-97.

[22] See, for example, the Anglican-Roman Catholic report "Authority in the Church," 1976, in *Growth in Agreement I*, 88-105; "Authority in the Church II" in *Growth in Agreement I*, 106-18; "The Gift of Authority," 1998, in *Growth in Agreement III*, 60-81; this is also echoed in §§83-84 of the Methodist-Roman Catholic document "Speaking the Truth in Love: Teaching Authority among Catholics and Methodists," in *Growth in Agreement III*, 163-164.

[23] Cf. *Baptism, Eucharist and Ministry*, section on Ministry, §23.

[24] Already at the first world conference on Faith and Order at Lausanne in 1927, the ordering of the churches in "episcopal," "presbyteral" and "congregational" systems was noted and the values underlying these three orders were "believed by many to be essential in the order of the Church." In H. N. Bate (ed.), *Faith and Order Proceedings of the World Conference: Lausanne, August 3-21, 1927*, London, Student Christian Movement, 1927, 379. Fifty-five years later, *Baptism, Eucharist and Ministry*, section on Ministry, Commentary on §26, cited this Lausanne text in justification of its affirmation that ordained ministry should be exercised in ways that are personal, collegial and communal.

Eucharist and Ministry as follows: "It should be *personal*, because the presence of Christ among his people can most effectively be pointed to by the person ordained to proclaim the Gospel and to call the community to serve the Lord in unity of life and witness. It should also be *collegial*, for there is need for a college of ordained ministers sharing in the common task of representing the concerns of the community. Finally, the intimate relationship between the ordained ministry and the community should find expression in a *communal* dimension where the exercise of the ordained ministry is rooted in the life of the community and requires the community's effective participation in the discovery of God's will and the guidance of the Spirit."[25]

53. One such exercise of oversight reflects that quality of the Church which might be termed "synodality" or "conciliarity." The word *synod* comes from the Greek terms *syn* (with) and *odos* (way) suggesting a "walking together." Both synodality and conciliarity signify that "each member of the Body of Christ, by virtue of baptism, has his or her place and proper responsibility" in the communion of the church.[26] Under the guidance of the Holy Spirit, the whole Church is synodal/conciliar, at all levels of ecclesial life: local, regional and universal. The quality of synodality or conciliarity reflects the mystery of the trinitarian life of God, and the structures of the Church express this quality so as to actualize the community's life as a communion. In the local eucharistic community, this quality is experienced in the profound unity in love and truth between the members and their presiding minister. In crucial situations synods have come together to discern the apostolic faith in response to doctrinal or moral dangers or heresies, trusting in the guidance of the Holy Spirit, whom Jesus promised to send after his return to the Father (cf. John 16:7.12-14). Ecumenical synods enjoyed the participation of leaders from the entire Church; their decisions were received by all as an acknowledgment of the important service they played in fostering and maintaining communion throughout the Church as a whole.[27] The churches currently have different views and practices about the participation and role of the laity in synods.

The authority of Ecumenical Councils

While most churches accept the doctrinal definitions of the early Ecumenical Councils as expressive of the teaching of the New Testament, some maintain that all post-biblical doctrinal decisions are open to revision, while others consider some doctrinal definitions to be normative and therefore irreformable expressions of the faith. Has ecumenical dialogue made possible a common assessment of the normativity of the teaching of the early Ecumenical Councils?

54. Wherever the Church comes together to take counsel and make important decisions, there is need for someone to summon and preside over the gathering for the sake of good order and to facilitate the process of promoting, discerning and articulating consensus. Those who preside are always to be at the service of those among whom they preside for the edification of

---

[25] *Baptism, Eucharist and Ministry,* section on "Ministry," §26.

[26] See Orthodox-Roman Catholic International Dialogue, "Ecclesial Communion, Conciliarity and Authority," §5, which notes that synodality may be taken as synonymous with conciliarity.

[27] An "ecumenical" council or synod would be one representing the whole Christian world. The first such council is universally recognized as that held at Nicaea in 325 to affirm the divinity of Christ in response to the new teaching of Arius, which denied the Son's equality with the Father. Churches differ on how many such councils have been held. On ecumenical councils and their authority, see, for example, the Lutheran-Orthodox "Authority in and of the Church: The Ecumenical Councils" (1993), in *Growth in Agreement III*, 12-14; the subsection "Councils and the Declaration of the Faith" of the Disciples-Roman Catholic, "Receiving and Handing on the Faith: The Mission and Responsibility of the Church," in *Growth in Agreement II*, 125-127; cf. also *Councils and the Ecumenical Movement*, Geneva, WCC, 1968.

the Church of God, in love and truth. It is the duty of the ones who preside to respect the integrity of local churches, to give voice to the voiceless and to uphold unity in diversity.

55. The word *primacy* refers to the custom and use, already recognized by the first ecumenical councils as an ancient practice, whereby the bishops of Alexandria, Rome and Antioch, and later Jerusalem and Constantinople, exercised a personal ministry of oversight over an area much wider than that of their individual ecclesiastical provinces. Such primatial oversight was not seen as opposed to synodality/conciliarity, which expresses more the collegial service to unity. Historically, forms of primacy have existed at various levels. According to canon 34 of the Apostolic Canons, which is expressive of the Church's self-understanding in the early centuries and is still held in honour by many, though not all, Christians today, the first among the bishops in each nation would only make a decision in agreement with the other bishops and the latter would make no important decision without the agreement of the first.[28] Even in the early centuries, the various ministries of primacy were plagued at times by competition between Church leaders. A primacy of decision-making (jurisdiction) and teaching authority, extending to the whole people of God, was gradually claimed by the Bishop of Rome on the basis of the relation of that local church to the apostles Peter and Paul. While acknowledged by many churches in the early centuries, its essential role and manner of exercise were matters of significant controversy. In recent years, the ecumenical movement has helped to create a more conciliatory climate in which a ministry in service to the unity of the whole Church has been discussed.

56. Partly because of the progress already recorded in bilateral and multilateral dialogues, the Fifth World Conference on Faith and Order raised the question "of a universal ministry of Christian unity."[29] In his encyclical *Ut Unum Sint,* Pope John Paul II quoted this text when he invited Church leaders and their theologians to "enter into patient and fraternal dialogue" with him concerning this ministry.[30] In subsequent discussion, despite continuing areas of disagreement, some members of other churches have expressed an openness to considering how such a ministry might foster the unity of local churches throughout the world and promote, not endanger, the distinctive features of their witness. Given the ecumenical sensitivity of this issue, it is important to distinguish between the essence of a ministry of primacy and any particular ways in which it has been or is currently being exercised. All would agree that any such personal primatial ministry would need to be exercised in communal and collegial ways.

57. There is still much work to be done to arrive at a convergence on this topic. At present Christians do not agree that a universal ministry of primacy is necessary or even desirable, although several bilateral dialogues have acknowledged the value of a ministry in service to the unity of the whole Christian community or even that such a ministry may be included in Christ's will

---

[28] This canon can be found at http://www.newadvent.org/fathers/3820.htm.

[29] §31.2 of "Report of Section II: Confessing the One Faith to God's Glory," in T. F. Best and G. Gassmann (eds.), *On the Way to Fuller Koinonia,* Geneva, WCC, 1994, 243.

[30] John Paul II, *Ut Unum Sint,* London, Catholic Truth Society, 1995, §96. A report entitled "Petrine Ministry" presents a synthesis and analysis of the various ecumenical dialogues which, up to 2001, had taken up the question of a ministry of primacy, as well as the responses given to John Paul's invitation to dialogue about this ministry. It grouped the central issues under four headings: scriptural foundations, *De iure divino* [whether such a ministry could be based upon God's will], universal jurisdiction (the exercise of authority or power within the Church), and papal infallibility. This preliminary report can be found in *Information Service,* N. 109 (2002/I-II), 29-42, and shows that the assessment of a "petrine ministry" differs significantly according to the particular tradition to which a Christian community belongs.

for his Church.[31] The lack of agreement is not simply between certain families of churches but exists within some churches. There has been significant ecumenical discussion of New Testament evidence about a ministry serving the wider unity of the Church, such as those of St Peter or of St Paul. Nevertheless, disagreements remain about the significance of their ministries and what they may imply concerning God's possible intention for some form of ministry in service to the unity and mission of the Church as a whole.

A universal ministry of unity

If, according to the will of Christ, current divisions are overcome, how might a ministry that fosters and promotes the unity of the Church at the universal level be understood and exercised?

---

[31] See the Anglican-Roman Catholic report "The Gift of Authority," in *Growth in Agreement III*, 60-81, and the Orthodox-Roman Catholic, "The Ecclesiological and Canonical Consequences of the Sacramental Nature of the Church."

CHAPTER IV

The Church: In and for the World

A. God's Plan for Creation: The Kingdom

58. The reason for the mission of Jesus is succinctly expressed in the words, "God so loved the world that he gave his only Son" (John 3:16). Thus the first and foremost attitude of God towards the world is love, for every child, woman and man who has ever become part of human history and, indeed, for the whole of creation. The kingdom of God, which Jesus preached by revealing the Word of God in parables and inaugurated by his mighty deeds, especially by the paschal mystery of his death and resurrection, is the final destiny of the whole universe. The Church was intended by God, not for its own sake, but to serve the divine plan for the transformation of the world. Thus, service (*diakonia*) belongs to the very being of the Church. The study document *Church and World* described such service in the following way: "As the body of Christ, the Church participates in the divine mystery. As mystery, it reveals Christ to the world by proclaiming the Gospel, by celebrating the sacraments (which are themselves called 'mysteries'), and by manifesting the newness of life given by him, thus anticipating the Kingdom already present in him."[1]

59. The Church's mission in the world is to proclaim to all people, in word and deed, the Good News of salvation in Jesus Christ (cf. Mk.16:15). Evangelization is thus one of the foremost tasks of the Church in obedience to the command of Jesus (cf. Matt. 28:18-20). The Church is called by Christ in the Holy Spirit to

---

[1] *Church and World: The Unity of the Church and the Renewal of Human Community*, Geneva, WCC, 1990, Chapter III, §21, page 27.

bear witness to the Father's reconciliation, healing and transformation of creation. Thus a constitutive aspect of evangelization is the promotion of justice and peace.

60. Today Christians are more aware of the wide array of different religions other than their own and of the positive truths and values they contain.[2] This occasions Christians to recall those gospel passages in which Jesus himself speaks positively about those who were "foreign" or "others" in relation to his listeners (cf. Matt. 8:11-12; Luke 7:9; 13:28-30). Christians acknowledge religious freedom as one of the fundamental dimensions of human dignity and, in the charity called for by Christ himself, they seek to respect that dignity and to dialogue with others, not only to share the riches of Christian faith but also to appreciate whatever elements of truth and goodness are present in other religions. In the past, when proclaiming the Gospel to those who had not yet heard it, due respect was not always given to their religions. Evangelization should always be respectful of those who hold other beliefs. Sharing the joyful news of the truth revealed in the New Testament and inviting others to the fullness of life in Christ is an expression of respectful love.[3] Within the contemporary context of increased awareness of religious pluralism, the possibility of salvation for those who do not explicitly believe in Christ and the relation between interreligious dialogue and the proclamation that Jesus is Lord have increasingly become topics of reflection and discussion among Christians.

Ecumenical response to religious pluralism

There remain serious disagreements within and between some churches concerning these issues. The New Testament teaches that God wills the salvation of all people (cf. 1 Tim. 2:4) and, at the same time, that Jesus is the one and only saviour of the world (cf. 1 Tim. 2:5 and Acts 4:12). What conclusions may be drawn from these biblical teachings regarding the possibility of salvation for those who do not believe in Christ? Some hold that, in ways known to God, salvation in Christ through the power of the Holy Spirit is possible for those who do not explicitly share Christian faith. Others do not see how such a view sufficiently corresponds to biblical passages about the necessity of faith and baptism for salvation. Differences on this question will have an impact upon how one understands and puts into practice the mission of the Church. Within today's context of increased awareness of the vitality of various religions throughout the world, how may the churches arrive at greater convergence about these issues and cooperate more effectively in witnessing to the Gospel in word and deed?

B. The Moral Challenge of the Gospel

61. Christians are called to repent of their sins, to forgive others and to lead sacrificial lives of service:

---

[2] On questions relating to this topic, see "Religious Plurality and Christian Self-Understanding" (2006), the result of a study process in response to suggestions made in 2002 at the WCC central committee to the three staff teams on Faith and Order, Inter-religious Relations, and Mission and Evangelism, available at:http://www.oikoumene.org/en/resources/documents/assembly/porto-alegre-2006/3-preparatory-and-background-documents/religious-plurality-and-christian-self-understanding.html. This statement follows the discussion of the relation between mission and world religions at the conference of the Commission on World Mission and Evangelism held in San Antonio in 1989. Because of its relevance to the general themes taken up in this chapter, some mention of interreligious relations will appear in each of its three sections.

[3] The "Charta Oecumenica" (2001) of the Conference of European Churches (CEC) and the Council of European Episcopal Conferences (CCEE), §2, states: "We commit ourselves to recognise that every person can freely choose his or her religious and church affiliation as a matter of conscience, which means not inducing anyone to convert through moral pressure or material incentive, but also not hindering anyone from entering

into conversion of his or her own free will. See also "Christian Witness in a Multi-Religious World: Recommendations for Conduct" of the Pontifical Council for Interreligious Dialogue, the World Council of Churches and the World Evangelical Alliance, approved on 28 January 2011, and available at: http://www.vatican.va/roman_curia/pontifical_councils/interelg/documents/rc_pc_interelg_doc_20111110_testimonianza-cristiana_en.html.

discipleship demands moral commitment. However, as St Paul so emphatically teaches, human beings are justified not through works of the law but by grace through faith (cf. Rom. 3:21-26; Gal. 2:19-21). Thus the Christian community lives within the sphere of divine forgiveness and grace, which calls forth and shapes the moral life of believers. It is of significant importance for the reestablishment of unity that the two communities whose separation marked the beginning of the Protestant Reformation have achieved consensus about the central aspects of the doctrine of justification by faith, the major focus of disagreement at the time of their division.[4] It is on the basis of faith and grace that moral engagement and common action are possible and should be affirmed as intrinsic to the life and being of the Church.

62. The ethics of Christians as disciples are rooted in God, the creator and revealer, and take shape as the community seeks to understand God's will within the various circumstances of time and place. The Church does not stand in isolation from the moral struggles of humankind as a whole. Together with the adherents of other religions as well as with all persons of good will, Christians must promote not only those individual moral values which are essential to the authentic realization of the human person but also the social values of justice, peace and the protection of the environment, since the message of the Gospel extends to both the personal and the communal aspects of human existence. Thus *koinonia* includes not only the confession of the one faith and celebration of common worship, but also shared moral values, based upon the inspiration and insights of the Gospel. Notwithstanding their current state of division, the churches have come so far in fellowship with one another that they are aware that what one does affects the life of others, and, in consequence, are increasingly conscious of the need to be accountable to each other with respect to their ethical reflections and decisions. As churches engage in mutual questioning and affirmation, they give expression to what they share in Christ.

63. While tensions about moral issues have always been a concern for the Church, in the world of today, philosophical, social and cultural developments have led to the rethinking of many moral norms, causing new conflicts over moral principles and ethical questions to affect the unity of the churches. At the same time, moral questions are related to Christian anthropology, and priority is given to the Gospel in evaluating new developments in moral thinking. Individual Christians and churches sometimes find themselves divided into opposing opinions about what principles of personal or collective morality are in harmony with the Gospel of Jesus Christ. Moreover, some believe that moral questions are not of their nature "church-dividing," while others are firmly convinced that they are.

Moral questions and the unity of the Church

Ecumenical dialogue at the multilateral and bilateral levels has begun to sketch out some of the parameters of the significance of moral doctrine and practice for Christian unity.[5] If present and future ecumenical dialogue is to serve both the mission and the unity of the Church, it is important that this dialogue explicitly address the challenges to convergence represented by contemporary moral issues. We invite the churches to explore

---

[4] See the Lutheran-Roman Catholic *Joint Declaration on the Doctrine of Justification,* Grand Rapids, Eerdmans, 2000.

[5] For example, the Anglican-Roman Catholic statement "Life in Christ: Morals, Communion and the Church," in *Growth in Agreement II,* 344-370; and the study document of the Joint Working Group of the World Council of Churches and the Roman Catholic Church, "The Ecumenical Dialogue on Moral Issues: Potential Sources of Common Witness or of Divisions" (1995), in *The Ecumenical Review* 48(2), April 1996, 143-154. For recent work on "Moral Discernment in the Churches" see Faith and Order Paper 215, WCC, Geneva, 2013.

these issues in a spirit of mutual attentiveness and support. How might the churches, guided by the Spirit, discern together what it means today to understand and live in fidelity to the teaching and attitude of Jesus? How can the churches, as they engage together in this task of discernment, offer appropriate models of discourse and wise counsel to the societies in which they are called to serve?

C. The Church in Society

64. The world that "God so loved" is scarred with problems and tragedies which cry out for the compassionate engagement of Christians. The source of their passion for the transformation of the world lies in their communion with God in Jesus Christ. They believe that God, who is absolute love, mercy and justice, can work through them, in the power of the Holy Spirit. They live as disciples of the One who cared for the blind, the lame and the leper, who welcomed the poor and the outcast, and who challenged authorities who showed little regard for human dignity or the will of God. The Church needs to help those without power in society to be heard; at times it must become a voice for those who are voiceless. Precisely because of their faith, Christian communities cannot stand idly by in the face of natural disasters which affect their fellow human beings or threats to health such as the HIV and AIDS pandemic. Faith also impels them to work for a just social order, in which the goods of this earth may be shared equitably, the suffering of the poor eased and absolute destitution one day eliminated. The tremendous economic inequalities that plague the human family, such as those in our day that often differentiate the global North from the global South, need to be an abiding concern for all the churches. As followers of the "Prince of Peace," Christians advocate peace, especially by seeking to overcome the causes of

war (principal among which are economic injustice, racism, ethnic and religious hatred, exaggerated nationalism, oppression and the use of violence to resolve differences). Jesus said that he came so that human beings may have life in abundance (cf. John 10:10); his followers acknowledge their responsibility to defend human life and dignity. These are obligations on churches as much as on individual believers. Each context will provide its own clues to discern what is the appropriate Christian response within any particular set of circumstances. Even now, divided Christian communities can and do carry out such discernment together and have acted jointly to bring relief to suffering human beings and to help create a society that fosters human dignity.[6] Christians will seek to promote the values of the kingdom of God by working together with adherents of other religions and even with those of no religious belief.

65. Many historical, cultural and demographic factors condition the relation between Church and state, and between Church and society. Various models of this relation based on contextual circumstances can be legitimate expressions of the Church's catholicity. It is altogether appropriate for believers to play a positive role in civic life. However, Christians have at times colluded with secular authorities in ways that condoned or even abetted sinful and unjust activities. The explicit call of Jesus that his disciples be the "salt of the earth" and the "light of the world" (cf. Matt. 5:13-16) has led Christians to engage with political and

---

[6] See, for example, the Reformed-Roman Catholic text "The Church as Community of Common Witness to the Kingdom of God," whose second chapter narrates cooperation between these churches concerning aboriginal rights in Canada, apartheid in South Africa and peace in Northern Ireland and whose third chapter describes the patterns of discernment used in each community, in PCPCU, *Information Service* N. 125 (2007/III), 121-138, and *Reformed World* 57(2/3), June-September 2007, 105-207.

economic authorities in order to promote the values of the kingdom of God, and to oppose policies and initiatives which contradict them. This entails critically analyzing and exposing unjust structures, and working for their transformation, but also supporting initiatives of the civil authorities that promote justice, peace, the protection of the environment and the care for the poor and the oppressed. In this way Christians are able to stand in the tradition of the prophets who proclaimed God's judgment on all injustice. This will very likely expose them to persecution and suffering. The servanthood of Christ led to the offering of his life on the cross and he himself foretold that his followers should expect a similar fate. The witness (*martyria*) of the Church will entail, for both individuals and for the community, the way of the cross, even to the point of martyrdom (cf. Matt. 10:16-33).

66. The Church is comprised of all socio-economic classes; both rich and poor are in need of the salvation that only God can provide. After the example of Jesus, the Church is called and empowered in a special way to share the lot of those who suffer and to care for the needy and the marginalized. The Church proclaims the words of hope and comfort of the Gospel, engages in works of compassion and mercy (cf. Luke 4:18-19) and is commissioned to heal and reconcile broken human relationships and to serve God in the ministry of reconciling those divided by hatred or estrangement (cf. 2 Cor. 5:18-21). Together with all people of goodwill, the Church seeks to care for creation, which groans to share in the freedom of the children of God (cf. Rom. 8:20-22), by opposing the abuse and destruction of the earth and participating in God's healing of broken relationships between creation and humanity.

CONCLUSION

67. The unity of the body of Christ consists in the gift of *koinonia* or communion that God graciously bestows upon human beings. There is a growing consensus that *koinonia*, as communion with the Holy Trinity, is manifested in three interrelated ways: unity in faith, unity in sacramental life, and unity in service (in all its forms, including ministry and mission). The liturgy, especially the celebration of the eucharist, serves as a dynamic paradigm for what such *koinonia* looks like in the present age. In the liturgy, the people of God experience communion with God and fellowship with Christians of all times and places. They gather with their presider, proclaim the Good News, confess their faith, pray, teach and learn, offer praise and thanksgiving, receive the Body and Blood of the Lord, and are sent out in mission.[1] St John Chrysostom spoke about two altars: one in the Church and the other among the poor, the suffering and those in distress.[2] Strengthened and nourished by the liturgy, the Church must continue the life-giving mission of Christ in prophetic and compassionate ministry to the world and in struggle against every form of injustice and oppression, mistrust and conflict created by human beings.

---

[1] The previous sentences largely repeat and paraphrase the statement from the 9th Forum on Bilateral Dialogues, held in Breklum, Germany, in March 2008. For the statement drawn up by this forum, see *The Ecumenical Review* 61(3), October 2009, 343-347; see also http://www.oikoumene.org/fileadmin/files/wcc-main/documents/p2/breklum-statement.pdf.
[2] St John Chrysostom, Homily 50, 3-4 on Matthew, in J. P. Migne, *Patrologia Graeca*, 58, 508-509.

68. One blessing of the ecumenical movement has been the discovery of the many aspects of discipleship which churches share, even though they do not yet live in full communion. Our brokenness and division contradict Christ's will for the unity of his disciples and hinder the mission of the Church. This is why the restoration of unity between Christians, under the guidance of the Holy Spirit, is such an urgent task. Growth in communion unfolds within that wider fellowship of believers that extends back into the past and forward into the future to include the entire communion of saints. The final destiny of the Church is to be caught up in the *koinonia*/communion of the Father, the Son and the Holy Spirit, to be part of the new creation, praising and rejoicing in God forever (cf. Rev. 21:1-4; 22:1-5).

69. "God did not send the Son into the world to condemn the world, but in order that the world might be saved through him" (John 3:17). The New Testament ends with the vision of a new heaven and a new earth, transformed by the grace of God (cf. Rev. 21:1-22:5). This new cosmos is promised for the end of history but is already present in an anticipatory way even now as the Church, upheld by faith and hope in its pilgrimage through time, calls out in love and worship "Come, Lord Jesus" (Rev. 22:20). Christ loves the Church as the bridegroom loves his bride (cf. Eph. 5:25) and, until the wedding feast of the lamb in the kingdom of heaven (cf. Rev. 19:7), shares with her his mission of bringing light and healing to human beings until he comes again in glory.

Historical Note

The Process Leading to *The Church: Towards a Common Vision*

The World Council of Churches describes itself as "a fellowship of churches which confess the Lord Jesus Christ as God and Savior according to the scriptures and therefore seek to fulfill together their common calling to the glory of the one God, Father, Son and Holy Spirit."[1] This "common calling" impels the churches to seek together convergence and greater consensus on the ecclesiological issues that yet divide them: What is the Church? What is the Church's role in God's cosmic design of recapitulation of all things in Jesus Christ?

During the past centuries, the way Christian churches have answered these questions has been marked by the fact that they live and do theology in an abnormal situation of ecclesial division. Therefore it is not surprising that a strong emphasis on ecclesiology – the theological question about the Church – accompanies the history of the modern ecumenical movement.

Thus, the 1927 World Conference on Faith and Order focused on seven theological subjects. One of them was dedicated to the nature of the Church;[2] a second dealt

---

[1] "Constitution and Rules of the World Council of Churches," in L. N. Rivera-Pagán (ed.), *God in Your Grace: Official Report of the Ninth Assembly of the World Council of Churches*, Geneva, WCC, 2007, 448.

[2] H. N. Bate (ed.), *Faith and Order: Proceedings of the World Conference – Lausanne, August 3-21, 1927*, New York, George H. Doran Co., 1927, esp. 463-466. *Reports of the World Conference on Faith and Order – Lausanne Switzerland August 3 to 21, 1927*, Boston, Faith and Order Secretariat, 1928, 19-24.

with the relation between the one Church we confess and the divided churches we experience in history. Based on the churches' responses to the findings of that meeting,[3] the organizers of the 1937 Second World Conference on Faith and Order proposed that the overarching theme for the next World Conference should be "The Church in the Purpose of God."[4] While the Second World Conference did not abide specifically with this theme, two of its five sections addressed core ecclesiological issues: "The Church of Christ and the Word of God" and "The Communion of Saints."[5] The 1937 World Conference concluded with the conviction that questions about the nature of the Church were at the root of most of the remaining dividing issues.[6]

In 1948 the recognition of oneness in Christ gave rise to a fellowship of still divided communions, made manifest in the establishment of the World Council of Churches. The report of that first WCC Assembly stated clearly that despite their oneness in Christ, the churches were fundamentally divided into two mutually inconsistent understandings of the Church, shaped by a more "active" or a more "passive" understanding of the role of the Church in God's salvation of the world.[7] It was in this new, complex ecumenical context — in which convergence on a lived Christology was helping the churches to recognize in each other vestiges of the one Church while remaining ecclesially and ecclesiologically divided — that the World Council of Churches' Commission on Faith and Order held its 1952 Third World Conference.

Unsurprisingly once again, the first of the three theological reports prepared for the Third World Conference[8] was based on a comprehensive exercise of comparative ecumenical ecclesiology. The fruits of this exercise were gathered in the book *The Nature of the Church,*[9] and this, in turn, was reflected in the second chapter of the Conference's final report entitled "Christ and His Church."[10] This was precisely the theme of the study report[11] presented, eleven years later, to the Section I of the 1963 Fourth World Conference on Faith and Order, called "The Church in the Purpose of God."[12]

The same emphasis on ecumenical ecclesiology has been demonstrated by the major statements about unity received by the assemblies of the WCC: the 1961 New Delhi statement on the unity of "all in each place"[13]; the 1975 Nairobi statement on the one Church as a conciliar fellowship[14]; the 1991 Canberra statement on

[3] For a selection of responses, see L. Dodgson (ed.), *Convictions: A Selection from the Responses of the Churches to the Report of the World Conference on Faith and Order, Held at Lausanne in 1927,* London, Student Christian Movement Press, 1934.

[4] L. Hodgson (ed.), *The Second World Conference on Faith and Order Held at Edinburgh, August 3-18, 1937,* London, Student Christian Movement Press, 1938, 5.

[5] Ibid., 228-235, 236-238.

[6] Cf. O. Tomkins, *The Church in the Purpose of God: An Introduction to the Work of the Commission on Faith and Order of the World Council of Churches,* Geneva, Faith and Order, 1950, 34.

[7] Cf. "The Universal Church in God's Design," in W. A. Visser 't Hooft (ed.), *The First Assembly of the World Council of Churches Held at Amsterdam August 22nd to September 4th, 1948,* London, SCM Press Ltd, 1949, 51-57.

[8] *The Church: A Report of a Theological Commission of the Faith and Order Commission of the World Council of Churches in Preparation for the Third World Conference on Faith and Order to Be Held at Lund, Sweden in 1952,* London, Faith and Order, 1951.

[9] R.N. Flew (ed.), *The Nature of the Church: Papers Presented to the Theological Commission Appointed by the Continuation Committee of the World Conference on Faith and Order,* London, SCM Press, 1952.

[10] *Report of the Third World Conference on Faith and Order, Lund, Sweden : August 15-28, 1952,* London, Faith and Order, 1952, 7-11.

[11] *Christ and the Church: Report of the Theological Commission for the Fourth World Conference on Faith and Order,* Geneva, WCC, 1963.

[12] P. C. Rodger and L. Vischer (eds.), *The Fourth World Conference on Faith and Order: Montreal, 1963,* New York, Association Press, 1964, 41-49.

[13] W. A. Visser 't Hooft (ed.), *The New Delhi Report: The Third Assembly of the World Council of Churches, 1961,* London, SCM Press, 1962, 116.

[14] D. M. Paton (ed.), *Breaking Barriers: Nairobi 1975 – The Official Report of the Fifth Assembly of the World Council of Churches, Nairobi, 23 November-10 December, 1975,* London-Grand Rapids, SPCK-Eerdmans, 1976, 60.

the unity of the Church as *koinonia*/communion[15]; and the 2006 Porto Alegre statement "Called to Be the One Church."[16] All these have been cumulative steps towards convergence and greater consensus on ecclesiology.

Compelled by the ecumenical vision of "all in each place" brought by the Holy Spirit into full visible unity in the apostolic faith, sacramental life, ministry, and mission, the Commission on Faith and Order dedicated a significant amount of its work in the years following the 1961 New Delhi Assembly to a convergence text on *Baptism, Eucharist and Ministry.*[17]

A significant moment in Faith and Order reflection on ecclesiology was the Fifth World Conference of 1993 at Santiago de Compostela, Spain. A number of factors shaped this World Conference with its theme "Towards *Koinonia* in Faith, Life and Witness." The first factor was the interpretation of the churches' responses to *Baptism, Eucharist and Ministry*, with its six published volumes of official responses.[18] The careful analysis of the 186 responses to BEM concluded with a list of several major ecclesiological themes that were requested for further study: the role of the Church in God's saving purpose; *koinonia*; the Church as a gift of the word of God (*creatura verbi*); the Church as mystery or sacrament of God's love for the world; the Church as the pilgrim people of God; the Church as prophetic sign and servant of God's coming kingdom.[19] The second factor shaping the 1993 Conference was the results of the

Faith and Order study process "Towards the Common Expression of the Apostolic Faith Today,"[20] which demonstrated an encouraging convergence about the entire doctrinal content of the Creed, including what it professes regarding the Church. The third factor was the study process on "The Unity of the Church and the Renewal of Human Community,"[21] which underlined the nature of the Church as sign and instrument of God's saving design for the world. And fourth were the ecclesiological challenges raised by the conciliar process on Justice, Peace and the Integrity of Creation.[22] As well, there was new ecumenical momentum created by the growing prominence of communion ecclesiology in the bilateral dialogues. These movements in the 1980s converged in the decision, taken by the Faith and Order Plenary Commission in 1989, to launch a new study on what was then called "The Nature and Mission of the Church – Ecumenical Perspectives on Ecclesiology."[23] The very theme of the Fifth World Conference – "Towards *Koinonia* in Faith, Life and Witness" – reflected all these study processes of the 1980s. While *The Church: Towards a Common Vision* takes its place within this long trajectory of Faith and Order reflection on the Church, fresh impetus was given to this work at the Fifth World Conference in 1993.

After several years of Faith and Order study and dialogue,

[15] M. Kinnamon (ed.), *Signs of the Spirit: Official Report Seventh Assembly – Canberra, Australia, 7-20 February 1991*, Geneva-Grand Rapids, WCC-Eerdmans, 1991, 172-174.

[16] L. N. Rivera-Pagán (ed.), *God, in your Grace: Official Report of the Ninth Assembly of the World Council of Churches*, Geneva, WCC, 2007, 255-261.

[17] *Baptism, Eucharist and Ministry,* Geneva, WCC, 1982.

[18] Cf. *Churches Respond to BEM* Geneva, WCC, 1986-1988, volumes I-VI.

[19] Cf. *Baptism, Eucharist & Ministry, 1982-1990: Report on the Process and Responses*, Geneva, WCC, 1990, 147-151.

[20] Cf. *Confessing the One Faith: An Ecumenical Explication of the Apostolic Faith as It Is Confessed in the Nicene-Constantinopolitan Creed (381)*, Faith and Order Paper 153, Geneva-Eugene, WCC-Wipf & Stock, 2010.

[21] Cf. *Church and World: The Unity of the Church and the Renewal of Human Community*, Faith and Order Paper 151, Geneva, WCC, 1990.

[22] "Final Document: Entering into Covenant Solidarity for Justice, Peace and the Integrity of Creation," in D.P. Niles (ed.), *Between the Flood and the Rainbow: Interpreting the Conciliar Process of Mutual Commitment (Covenant) to Justice, Peace and the Integrity of Creation*, Geneva, WCC, 1992, 164-190; cf. T. F. Best & M. Robra (eds.), *Ecclesiology and Ethics: Ecumenical Ethical Engagement, Moral Formation, and the Nature of the Church*. Geneva, WCC, 1997.

[23] Cf. G. Gassmann, "The Nature and Mission of the Church: Ecumenical Perspectives," in T. F. Best (ed.), *Faith and Order 1985-1989: The Commission Meeting at Budapest 1989*, Geneva, WCC, 1990, esp. 202-204, 219.

an initial result of the Ecclesiology study was published in 1998 under the title *The Nature and Purpose of the Church*.[24] Its status as a provisional text was expressed in the subtitle: *A Stage on the Way to a Common Statement*. It is a text of six chapters: "The Church of the Triune God," "The Church in History," "The Church as *Koinonia* (Communion)," "Life in Communion," "Service in and for the World," and "Following Our Calling: From Converging Understandings to Mutual Recognition." Responses to this text were received from churches, ecumenical organizations, and regional councils of churches, academic institutions and individuals. Many appreciative comments were complemented by some points of constructive criticism. For example, it seemed that *The Nature and Purpose of the Church* needed further integration: how could the theme of the Church as Communion be treated apart from the chapter on the Church of the Triune God? Furthermore, some issues were considered missing: for instance, there was no section on teaching authority and the topic of mission seemed to receive little attention. As well, the World Conference at Santiago had called for a study on "the question of a universal ministry of Christian unity,"[25] which was not reflected in the text. Significantly, in his 1995 encyclical letter on commitment to ecumenism, *Ut Unum Sint*, inviting dialogue about the ministry of the Bishop of Rome, Pope John Paul II cited the Faith and Order recommendation from Santiago.[26]

When sufficient time had been allowed for the responses to come in, the commission set out revising its ecclesiology text, producing a new draft entitled *The Nature and Mission of the Church,*[27] which was presented to the 2006 WCC Assembly held in Porto Alegre, Brazil. Seeking to incorporate the suggestions from the various responses, it comprises four chapters: "The Church of the Triune God," "The Church in History," "The Life of Communion in and for the World," and "In and For the World." The first chapter integrated much of the biblical material on the nature of the Church as people of God, body of Christ and temple of the Holy Spirit, with biblical insights on the church as communion (*koinonia*) and on the mission of the Church as servant of the Kingdom and with the creedal affirmation of the Church as One, Holy, Catholic and Apostolic. The second chapter on history highlighted the problems that afflict the churches in their present division: how can diversity be harmonized with unity and what makes for legitimate diversity? How do the churches understand the local church and how is it related to all other churches? What are the historic and ongoing issues that divide Christians? The third chapter highlighted the elements necessary for communion between the churches, such as apostolic faith, baptism, eucharist, ministry, *episkopé*, councils and synods, with the themes of universal primacy and authority now included. A final chapter more briefly explored the Church's service to the world in assisting those who suffer, defending the oppressed, witnessing to the moral message of the Gospel, working for justice, peace and the protection of the environment, and generally seeking to promote a human society more in keeping with the values of the Kingdom of God.

This revised text on ecclesiology was also subtitled "A Stage on the Way to a Common Statement," and it too was sent to the churches for response. Over

---

[24] *The Nature and Purpose of the Church: A Stage on the Way to a Common Statement*, Geneva, WCC, 1998.

[25] T. F. Best and G. Gassmann (eds.), *On the Way to Fuller Koinonia: Official Report of the Fifth World Conference on Faith and Order*, Geneva, WCC, 1994, 243.

[26] *Encyclical Letter Ut Unum Sint of the Holy Father, John Paul II, on Commitment to Ecumenism*, Rome, Libreria Editrice Vaticana, 1995, §89.

[27] *The Nature and Mission of the Church: A Stage on the Way to a Common Statement*, Faith and Order Paper 198, WCC, Geneva, 2005.

eighty responses were received, although only around thirty were specifically from the churches. Most of the responses from the churches, academic and ecumenical institutes, and significantly from missionary organizations, expressed satisfaction that the mission of the Church was given greater prominence, even having a place in the title. Other comments were concerned that the use of the two words – *nature* and *mission* – would obscure the fact that the Church is by its very nature missionary. To assist the Ecclesiology Working Group in assessing the responses to *The Nature and Mission of the Church*, Faith and Order staff prepared detailed summaries and initial analyses of every response.

Three particularly significant steps were taken in evaluating *The Nature and Mission of the Church*. First, the Plenary Commission of Faith and Order, with its 120 members representing the various churches, held its meeting in Crete in October 2009. This gathering brought together many who were participating in Faith and Order for the first time and the meeting was structured in such a way as to maximize the input of the commissioners to the three study projects of Faith and Order, especially the ecclesiology study. A number of plenary sessions assessed *The Nature and Mission of the Church*. [28] A major direction from the Plenary Commission was to shorten the text and to make it more contextual, more reflective of the lives of the churches throughout the world, and more accessible to a wider readership. Twelve working groups discussed *The Nature and Mission of the Church*, and produced detailed evaluations on the text.[29]

Second, in June 2010 at Holy Etchmiadzin, Armenia, the Faith and Order Standing Commission decided that after a careful examination of the responses to *The Nature and Mission of the Church,* and the evaluations of the text from the meeting of the Plenary Commission in Crete, the time was right to begin a final revision. A drafting committee was appointed with theologians coming from the Anglican, Catholic, Lutheran, Methodist, Orthodox, and Reformed traditions; the two co-moderators came from the Methodist and Orthodox traditions respectively.

Third, the commission was aware of a significant lacuna in the responses process: there was as yet no substantial response from the Eastern and Oriental Orthodox churches. Accordingly, a major inter-Orthodox consultation was held Aghia Napa, Cyprus, in the Holy Metropolitanate of Constantia, in March of 2011, which included 40 delegated theologians from ten Eastern Orthodox and three Oriental Orthodox churches. The consultation produced an extensive evaluation of *The Nature and Mission of the Church*. A major suggestion was to integrate more clearly the material on baptism, eucharist and ministry into the presentation of what is essential to the life of the Church. The consultation and its report became a significant component of the next meeting of the Ecclesiology Working Group, and hence played a unique role in the process that led to the new text.

Extensive analysis of the responses continued at the first meeting of the drafting committee in Geneva in late November, 2010. The process was given fresh impetus after the inter-Orthodox consultation in early March, 2011. A meeting of the Ecclesiology Working Group which took place in Columbus, Ohio, USA, later that month produced a new draft version of the text that was presented to the Standing Commission of Faith and Order in Gazzada, Italy, in July 2011. Many comments were received from the commissioners,

[28] Cf. John Gibaut (ed.), *Called to Be the One Church: Faith and Order at Crete*, Geneva, WCC, 2012, 147-193.
[29] Cf. ibid. 207-231.

mostly quite favorable but suggesting that the text needed to emphasize more clearly ways in which progress had been made towards greater convergence, especially on the ministry, and in particular in bilateral agreed statements, as well as recent Faith and Order work, such as the study text *One Baptism: Towards Mutual Recognition.*[30]

This request was addressed by strengthening some of the formulations and supporting them with notes which substantiate the progress achieved towards convergence. Subsequently, another version was prepared by the drafting committee at the Bossey Ecumenical Institute in Switzerland, in December 2011. The drafting committee was much aided by reflections coming from staff of the WCC's Commission on World Mission and Evangelism. The resulting text was then submitted to four outside ecumenical experts for a fresh evaluation; their suggestions were evaluated and incorporated by the drafting committee and presented to the Ecclesiology Working Group in a meeting held in Freising, Germany, late March 2012. On the basis of the discussions and reactions to the text at the Freising meeting, the Ecclesiology Working Group arrived at a final draft to be presented to the Faith and Order Standing Commission.

In Penang, Malaysia, on 21 June 2012, the final text was presented to the Standing Commission, which unanimously approved it as a convergence statement with the title *The Church: Towards a Common Vision.* Thus the present text is not a stage on the way to a further common statement; it is the common statement to which its previous versions – *The Nature and Purpose of the Church* and *The Nature and Mission of the Church* – were directed. *The Church: Towards a Common Vision* brings to completion a particular stage of Faith and Order reflection on the Church. The commission believes that its reflection has reached such a level of maturity that it can be identified as a convergence text, that is, a text of the same status and character as the 1982 *Baptism, Eucharist and Ministry.* As such, it is being sent to the churches as a common point of reference in order to test or discern their own ecclesiological convergences with one another, and so to serve their further pilgrimage towards the manifestation of that unity for which Christ prayed. The central committee of the World Council of Churches at its meeting in Crete, Greece, in early September, 2012, received *The Church: Towards a Common* Vision and commended it to the member churches for study and formal response.

---

[30] *One Baptism: Towards Mutual Recognition,* Geneva, WCC, 2011.